The Druid Way

A Journey through an Ancient Landscape

revised edition

with foreword

by Cairisthea Worthington

Philip Ca

By the same author

The DruidCraft Tarot (with Stephanie Carr-Gomm)
Druid Mysteries – Ancient Wisdom for the 21st Century
Druidcraft – the Magic of Wicca & Druidry
In The Grove of the Druids – the Druid Teachings of Ross Nichols
The Druid Animal Oracle (with Stephanie Carr-Gomm)

The Druid Way

A Journey through an Ancient Landscape

revised edition
with foreword
by Cairisthea Worthington

Philip Carr-Gomm

Thoth Publications
Loughborough, Leicestershire

Second Edition

A CIP catalogue record for this book is available from the British Library.

Cover design by Avanson Design

Printed and bound in the USA

Published by Thoth Publications
64, Leopold Street Loughborough, LE11 5DN

ISBN 978-1-870450-62-1
Web address www.thoth.co.uk
email: enquiries@thoth.co.uk

This whole book is a delight. It is the diary of a sacred journey, through sacred space, and through the heart and mind, as well as a useful practical guide to the countryside and its associations and history. It is a book to use and to keep and to remember.

Asphodel, review in Wood & Water

Philip Carr-Gomm's intelligence – not unlike Andrew Harvey's – has a bright, mercurial and energising quality that immediately stimulates interest and attention. Far superior to a rote historical study, his book is an experiential pilgrimage, a first-hand account that could only be charted by someone as sufficiently steeped in the ideas from the inside of his skin as is Philip. And here is where it begins: high on the downlands above Lewes on the South Downs Way, as he stands on Itford Hill at the outset of his circular journey of excursion and return. From here, in twenty-one chapters, he unfolds a compelling narrative that is both story and exploration, memory and discourse, homily and lyric exposition, coloured with his own immediate psychic perception.

'I plead very guilty to being indeed my own ancestor', as Nuinn is quoted in the book...and what is everywhere present here is the presence of the past that the whole landscape resonates, and that Philip unearths, naming original place names, tracking lost paths gone to grass and cut through by our present roads – and he does so with a sense of detail reminiscent of Gilbert White, though his canvas is larger.

Jay Ramsay, review in Resurgence

The Druid Way makes an interesting departure from the routine glut of Paganism-by-numbers manuals. Instead it describes one person's journey in the countryside of southern England that evolves into any-person's journey of self-discovery, and discovery of the Goddess of the Land. This is refreshingly in touch with the roots of our primal traditions, containing much of interest on the lore of the Land: giants, dragons, ancestors, birds, trees and the seasons. Our relationship with the Goddess is explored in depth, with particular insights into the misdirection of male energy.

Martin Wood, review in Pagan Dawn

The Druid Way passes beyond the rural appeal of these writers by the interweaving of place with the author's own druidic tradition. Here is one who has walked the land and understood its secrets through every sense. Here there is no urging to try out techniques you don't understand the need or purpose of, no exhortation to join or become anything that you are not; just a strong affirmation to explore the land as the person that you are, to be a soul on pilgrimage through life itself, listening to the voices of the heart within you and the earth beneath your feet.

This timely book speaks to all who seek for the roots of their belonging in the land in which they live. It provides inspiration, soul-food and encouragement to those who long to be part of the richer life of this beautiful planet.

Caitlin Matthews, review in Touchstone

It took some time to adjust to the writer's fusion of vision, poetry and academic fact. Philip Carr-Gomm's style is not to present fixed dogmas or structures of belief but to wander freely among ideas and images, allowing great play to the subconscious mind.

The seed of the journey is set on the occasion of a death at the Winter Solstice, initiating an exploration of Life and Death within the Celtic year. The outward journey, at Imbolc, is full of exploration and growth on many levels. It ends with the discovery of the Harvest God's wound. Fittingly the return journey is made at Lughnasadh. In the time between, there has been a death and a birth.

This superficially simple book contains an underlying complexity which provokes disagreement as well as insight. It is an interesting contribution towards the constantly growing recognition of the older forms of the land, yearly negated by the tarmac chain-mail which, paradoxically, denies access to Place and the related portion of our collective cultures. The lasting image of the book is the sexually ambivalent figure of Wilmington, the empty space enclosed by the chalk lines, a creative metaphor for the path of those inspired by indigenous spirituality.

Talking Stick magazine

Contents

PREFACE

When I was asked to write a book about the Druid Way I planned to write a straightforward description of the history, beliefs and practices of the Druid Tradition. But a little before I was due to begin writing, I was guided towards an experience of the Druid Way that resulted in an entirely different book.

Central to Druidry is the idea that we should 'listen to the land' - that it can speak to us and guide us if we are able to open ourselves to it. One night I was lucky enough to hear the land speak to me - or so it seemed - and I decided to follow its invitation to walk through the local landscape in a spirit of openness and acceptance, so that I could write about the Druid Way not from an objective point of view, but from the inside - from the point of view of someone walking this Way at a particular time in a particular place. The result is not a manual or even a description of Druidry (these are available elsewhere and references are offered in the Notes) instead it is an account of one person's experience of walking in the world, listening to the ancestral voices that speak through the landscape.

Preface to the Second Edition

I would love to live
Like a river flows,
Carried by the surprise
Of its own unfolding.
John O'Donohue

Sometimes books seem to have a life of their own, and no sooner was this one published thirteen years ago, than it walked out into the world and began inspiring some people and upsetting others. As a result, to my surprise, I found myself giving national newspaper and radio interviews, and appearing on television for the first time. I had thought *The Druid Way* would be a book of very limited appeal, perhaps being of interest to a Sussex audience, but instead I discovered that readers, wherever they live, are passionate about their local landscape and history, and that in writing about my local area, I had somehow managed to inspire them to explore their own.

I upset some readers because I included a chapter discussing the two religions that Britain has given to the world: Druidism and Wicca, and quoted some controversial opinions voiced by other writers. Since then I have developed this subject in *Druidcraft – the Magic of Wicca & Druidry*, *The Rebirth of Druidry*, and in *The DruidCraft Tarot* to such a degree that the original chapter in this book felt redundant, and I have accordingly removed it.

Thirteen years on, the concrete shaft in the Tump mentioned at the beginning of Chapter Three, has still not been removed, despite a valiant attempt by Dr.Andrew Stirling, which included a series of letters to the local paper to argue for the removal of this 'hazardous and unsightly socket'. Nevertheless, friends did manage to organise a 'Long Man' conference at Subud House in Lewes, which drew together speakers from Christian, Druid and Wiccan perspectives.

Awareness of the Long Man seemed to grow after the appearance of the book – most of this quite coincidentally. In 1994, to protest against the Tory government's road-building madness, the cartoonist Steve Bell created a hill figure near Brighton of John Major wearing only underpants, with a traffic cone on his head, and later the girls of Roedean painted a replica of the Long Man on the school lawn, generously restoring his manhood, and ensuring that helicopters were soon flying overhead to photograph their handiwork for the papers. It cannot have been a coincidence that their history teacher was Rodney Castleden, author of *The Wilmington Giant.* The Lewes brewery, Harvey's, began producing 'Long Man' ale, and local artists lobbied the council to create a new hill figure, this time of a goddess, overlooking the town.

The suggestions I made in the chapter entitled 'The Slopes of the Galedin' found support, when in 1997, local archaeologist John Bleach published a paper in the Sussex Archaeological Collections, which revealed the existence, in ancient times, of four mounds in the town, which if included with the three existing mounds, suggests that Lewes was home to at least seven sacred mounds. In an appendix to John Bleach's article, Richard Coates develops his ideas on the meaning of the name Lewes, which he reasons could be either 'tumuli' or 'slopes'.

I mention in the book that the only major 'blot on the landscape' of Lewes is the office block of the East Sussex County Council, and it was heartening to read recently of a desire amongst residents to have the offices demolished and rebuilt.

As the millennium approached, there seemed to be a collective need for reparations to be made – a clearing of the slate. Although John Howard, Prime Minister of Australia, went against the prevailing mood, and refused to apologise to the Aboriginal community, the Pope did apologise for some of the misdeeds of the Catholic church, and the town of Lewes made reparations for the blunder it made (mentioned in Chapter Thirteen) when it refused to exhibit Rodin's Kiss that had been donated to it by the wealthy art collector Edward Warren. As the world entered the 21st century, Lewes feted the return of the Kiss from the Tate gallery in London, and held a Rodin Festival which included performances of a play about the statue and its relationship to the town, and an exhibition of Rodin's work. Harvey's took the opportunity to produce another ale, this time called 'The Kiss'.

The Sussex Archaeological Society made tentative plans to hold a Long Man festival, and I began discussions with playwrights John Agard and Fiona Graham with the idea of developing a play about the discovery of the Long Man which, together with an art exhibition, lectures and poetry recitals, could become part of the Brighton Festival. So far neither of these projects has materialised. Perhaps they will one day, and perhaps one day too, the sculptural dream of Eric Gill and Jacob Epstein, to create a circle of giant dancing figures in the Sussex countryside will be realised.

John Agard did, however, develop a poem of his about the Long Man into part of a libretto which was performed at Glyndebourne, and we held a 'mini-festival' one afternoon in the village hall at Wilmington, with performances of Long Man poetry by John Agard and Grace Nichols.

Two Druid groups formed in the area, drawing their inspiration from the landscape around the Long Man: the Anderida Grove and the Avronelle Seed Group of the Order of Bards Ovates & Druids. The Anderida group also began holding open gatherings to celebrate the eight festivals beside the Long Man, and in 2003, with the cooperation of the Sussex Archaeological Society, and with paint donated by the Order, members of both local groups re-painted the concrete blocks which outline the figure.

In 2004 the Arts Council funded the publication of a novel by Somerset Bard Kevan Manwaring, *The Long Woman*, which movingly explores the theme of the sacred landscape of England and France, as it is explored by an antiquarian's widow between the wars. A key section of the book reproduces the antiquarian's journal entry for his visit to the Long Man.

A charity walk following part of the route taken in *The Druid Way*, from Lewes to the Long Man, has already been undertaken, and another took place in the summer of 2005, to raise funds for the charities Trees for Life, and Care for the Wild, and for the Sacred Grove Planting Programme of the Order of Bards Ovates & Druids.

Looking back it is surprising to see how much activity this enigmatic figure in the landscape has inspired. Perhaps it is because although the figure seems to be simply holding two staves, we feel that something more is going on – that a doorway is being held open, and we are simultaneously being invited in and at the same time being barred from entry. The figure challenges us and evokes in us a longing to journey to the Otherworld that lies beyond the staves, behind the open doorway…

Introduction

In Druidry the sacred journey of self-discovery is intimately linked with our need for reconnection to the natural world, the wisdom of the Ancestors and the turning wheel of the year. The world of nature becomes a wise teacher who inspires the bard, the mystic and the philosopher. Celtic art, poetry and stories abound with references to the landscape and the natural world, whose wildness and beauty touches the soul and allows the experience of the sacred to flow through daily life.

The world of nature is the Muse of all those who resonate with the Celtic Spirit. The presence of the Ancestors in the land, and the changing face of the landscape through the turning wheel of the year represent deep sources of wisdom.

These three strands of inspiration – the cycle of the year, the power of the ancestors and of nature – combine in *The Druid Way* to create a truly magical book. Through one man's journey along the ancient trackways of Southern Britain we are connected to the living Spirit of the Druid Tradition. Philip Carr-Gomm journeys through the landscape in a way few people do today. He journeys consciously; allowing landscape, weather, myth, history, meditation, poetry and the daily events of his life to weave a magical and empowering way of experiencing the world around him.

All spiritual paths have their sacred symbolism and one of the most potent symbols is the spiral. The whole universe is a pattern of spirals from the tiny neutrino to the vast wheeling galaxies. The Old Ones of the Isles of Britain carved this powerful symbol in stone and created mounds with spiralling pathways that created vortices of power in the landscape.

Philip begins the journey described in this book at one such mound, the Tump in Lewes, and to this mound he returns at a significant time.

The memory of that time will be with me for the rest of my own journey through life, for it was the moment when my daughter Lucie left this world to travel beyond our sight and into the Other Worlds. Nestling within the pages of this book is a chapter that speaks with love and honesty about her death in the springtime of the year and of her life.

There is something about a child's pure and shining life force that reminds us that human life is sacred, and when that purity and light suddenly leaves this world it is utterly shocking. We are truly bereft.

But death is part of life; part of the journey we all take in this world no matter how desperately we sometimes wish it were otherwise.

During the days that followed her death I felt as though I was travelling to the centre of a vortex: my spirit, intimately linked to my daughter, was trying to follow her. At the centre of the vortex I could go no further. Lucie's journey had taken her beyond my reach; and so I rested there at the gateway between life and death. Suddenly I was overwhelmed by a terrible grey deep sorrow, so powerful that I felt as though I was suffocating. After a while, its strength waned and I began to experience the most wonderful sense of joy - the joy of knowing and loving my beautiful daughter.

For a space of time the feelings of joy and sorrow ebbed and flowed like the rhythm of the sea on a lonely shore. I let go and allowed myself to feel all there was to feel in this place of joy and sorrow, life and death, light and dark. And then all at once I knew with absolute certainty that there was no separation between these seemingly opposite dynamics;

where joy was, sorrow was also; where there was life, there was death; without darkness there was no light. I felt safe and protected in this place of healing, drifting in the waters of the womb of the Great Mother, the giver and taker of Life. And what allowed me to stay in that place of healing was the sense that I knew my way out whenever I needed to leave. The wisdom of the Druid tradition had become a map that was able to guide me through the most harrowing time of my life. Its wisdom and knowledge would guide me back to my own time even from the gateway between life and death.

The Ancestors had carved the pathway in spiral patterns, and had formed massive mounds, which carried the spiralling paths that are the images of the sacred gateways between the worlds. And it was to one of these mounds that Philip instinctively turned when he heard of Lucie's passing.

In the Autumn that followed that dreadful time, I sat one day leaning against the old apple tree in my garden and thought about the times Lucie had pushed her wheelbarrow from the stable at the back of the house, through the garden to the paddock beyond the trees. And suddenly a question arose in my mind. To find the answer I felt I needed to connect with the spirits of the garden, so I allowed myself to drift into a state of reverie, until I became aware of the presence of the spirit of the old apple tree. Aware of how devastated we had all been, I asked the apple tree, 'Were you affected by her death?' 'No,' came the reply, 'we were affected by her life'. For some time I let this powerful reflection drift deeper into my awareness.

In the natural world, the cycle of life and death flows in an ever changing and dynamic dance through the seasons, the decades, the millennia. Nothing is static. Nothing stays the same forever. It is when we, as human beings, try to hold on to that which needs to change that we feel distress and conflict.

Death is a part of life, and of course we feel overwhelming grief and loss when a loved one dies; that is human, that is natural. We are told that it takes time to 'get over' such a loss, but I have discovered that that statement is wrong. We never 'get over' it. Instead we learn to live with the fact of it. But what helps to ease the pain is the knowledge that everyone has their own journey, a journey that they have a sacred right to take. But sometimes that journey takes our loved ones from us before we are ready to part with them. My daughter needed to continue her journey beyond this world, and our love and blessings would go with her always. And just as the apple tree and the garden had been affected by her life, I would honour and remember with joy all that she had been, all that she had taught me, all that she had brought into this world just by being herself - and I have to say her sometimes wild and unruly self! Our journey continues beyond this one single human lifetime, we travel in and out of this physical world experiencing all that a greater Life has to offer: the sorrow and the joy, the light and the darkness, summer and winter, life and death. The life force, that is depicted in the sacred mounds as spiralling pathways, carries our spirits in and out of this world many, many times giving us the opportunity to learn and develop as wise and compassionate beings.

Recently I gave a Druid workshop here in Scotland. One of the participants was a man who had read *The Druid Way* after its first publication in 1993, and it had touched a great loss in his own life. He was a father whose daughter Joanna had died tragically some years before my own. As the workshop progressed he spoke of how, as a man, he had been expected to 'put a brave face on it', 'keep a stiff upper lip', and how in the attempt to do this, he had never been able to let the healing process begin. His 'winter of despair' had lasted for far too many years. But as we worked that day with the understanding of the cyclical nature of life, he felt something begin to shift and the possibility of healing begin. The wisdom that flows from our sacred relationship with the natural world tells us that nothing stays the same: everything changes, and as Druids we know ourselves to be part of the natural cycle of life and death. As parents we could grieve. As Druids we would honour the journey our children had taken.

When the time is right, each one of us will journey beyond this world. Our physical body will return to the earth, but our spirit will flow with the great river of life through space and time in an ever-changing dance of life. In Druidry we seek to become a conscious and creative partner in the dance. And the first steps are taken in the life that we have right now. Human life and the life of the land are entwined in a sacred relationship that is honoured in Druidry. And by looking with new eyes at the world around us, listening to the songs of our Ancestors, discovering the wisdom inherent in nature, and respecting the sacred journey of all those who travel with us, our own life will become truly empowered.

Cairisthea Worthington
10th April 2006
Kirkcudbright, Scotland

This book is dedicated to

Boris Nikolov who walked through the gateway in Winter

and Lucie Worthington who walked through the gateway in Spring

You do not have to be good.
You do not have to walk on your knees
for a hundred miles through the desert, repenting.
You only have to let the soft animal of your body
love what it loves.
Tell me about despair, yours, and I will tell you mine.
Meanwhile the world goes on.
Meanwhile the sun and the clear pebbles of the rain
are moving across the landscapes,
over the prairies and the deep trees,
the mountains and the rivers.
Meanwhile the wild geese, high in the clean blue air,
are heading home again.
Whoever you are, no matter how lonely,
the world offers itself to your imagination,
calls to you like the wild geese, harsh and exciting -
over and over announcing your place
in the family of things.

Mary Oliver

The Dun

Follow your bliss.

Joseph Campbell

A hawk flying over the Downlands would have had an even better view. But I was almost as high as the hawk and could see almost as far... There to the south was the sea, grey and silvery. There to the west was a long arm of the Downs, stretching from the mouth of the river Ouse at Newhaven to Swanborough Hill in the far distance.

Over to the North-East stood Mount Caburn facing the sea-horizon like a warrior. I was standing on Itford Hill, 540 feet above sea level, on the South Downs Way - an ancient track that leads from Eastbourne to Winchester. In the old days, further tracks led from Winchester to Stonehenge.

With the sea at my back, and with the Downs, the Dun, beneath me and to either side, I could see the starting point of my journey - way below and straight ahead. There, in a gap in the Downs, lay the city of Lugh, guarding this entry point to the Weald of Sussex.

I could see the river meandering from Newhaven to Lewes via the Brookland basin - an area of flat land that would once have been a floodplain or lagoon. And there rising out of the basin was Lewes itself - the town on the hill, crowned by its castle.

The sun was shining brilliantly and just at the edge of the town, facing due south directly beneath the castle, was the Tump - the sacred mound that was responsible one midwinter night for sending me on this journey...

The Light of Arthur

We have to leave the Garden of Eden before we can start the journey to the Heavenly Jerusalem. It is ironic that the two are the same place but the journey must be made.

Robert A Johnson

It was midwinter night. A group of about a dozen of us stood at the edge of the bowling green, gazing up at the strange flat-topped hill that was lit only by the moon. We then began to climb the path that winds snake-like around the hill, until we reached the summit.

There, on the flat surface of the hill-top, we held hands in a circle, swayed in the wind, greeted the stars and the moon, the hills on the horizon, and the town that lay beneath us. Then, one by one, we tipped the contents of the bags we had been carrying into a hole in the centre of the circle. Someone bent down and placed a sprig of mistletoe on the earth, and then slowly one by one we walked down the snake-path to the bowling green, and then crossed the road and railway bridge to travel home.

It was December 22nd, the evening of the winter solstice, called Alban Arthan, The Light of Arthur, in the Druid Tradition.

That night, at twenty-two minutes to midnight, a close friend died.

The next evening, I went back to that same hill, stood alone at the summit, and said a prayer for him and thought about his life, and the wisdom, joy and kindness he had given to so many people. I then walked down the snake-path. As I reached the base of the hill, I leant against its steep sides with the palms of my hands.

Suddenly the whole hill was ablaze with light. 'Nothing is what it appears to be.' She told me, 'Spirit is everywhere. Splendour and love and power are everywhere. The land is sacred. Go on a journey. Start here - where you live.'

The Spiral Of Beginnings

And Taliesin shall be
in many wonderful shapes,
a grain of wheat and a hare
  sown and running
while there are fields, and the spirit of men
leaping alive at a harvest, or silver in the waters of time.

Nuinn

I had moved from one city of Lugh, the ancient Celtic god of light, to another the year previously. For nearly forty years Caer Llundain, the ancient city of London, had been my home, but the previous Winter I had moved to Lewes, the county town of East Sussex, in south-eastern England.

Although Lewes is an attractive town, with picturesque cottages, narrow lanes and a medieval castle, it is, like many English towns, plagued with heavy traffic and I had never really felt at home there.

That midwinter night, we as a group celebrated the Druid festival of Alban Arthan, and at the same time took one small step towards repairing the damage others had done to their local environment. We had carried bags of earth to the top of the Lewes Tump, and filled a hole that had been left by Christians who each year erect a large cross on the hill at Easter time. The hole had become a trap for refuse, and besides looking ugly, acted as a dangerous snare for unwary visitors. That night we 'took the law into our own hands' and it felt good.

Somehow it signalled a change. From not feeling at home in the town, I began to feel I belonged. And paradoxically to feel fully at home I now needed to leave it. I needed to take a journey - to rediscover the sacred landscape that surrounded me - to rediscover the sacred in life that the modern age has tried so hard to destroy.

This, it seems, is the central problem of our age. In researching this book, I turned to Hilaire Belloc's *The Old Road* and H.J.Massingham's *Through the Wilderness.*

Belloc wrote of his desire to walk the old track of the North Downs Way, so that he could 'forget the vileness' of his own time. Massingham wrote of his wish to build a house facing the Downs, as a 'desire for stability against the blind tides of our times' remarking that 'a fatalism...set in motion by our own deeds and undeeds, has taken possession of our lives'. Belloc's book was published in 1911, and Massingham's in 1935. Belloc found his contemporary world a problem before the First World War, and Massingham before the Second. Both found themselves struggling with the problems brought about by the 'modern' world and they didn't even know about gas chambers and nuclear winters and holes in the fabric of the sky.

But we do, and the central problem for us now is: How do we change our world, before it's too late? or in another way: How do we stop changing our world, before it's too late?

In addressing this problem, this book attempts to unite two approaches that are apparently widely different in stance and methodology, but which are closer in many ways than at first appears. These two approaches are those of the ancient sacred tradition of this land, Druidry, and the newer discipline of psychology.

With psychological understanding we discover that one of our central problems is one of alienation: from ourselves, from others around us, and from the world of nature. Psychotherapy began the task of putting some of the different parts of ourselves back in touch with each other, so that our minds were no longer alienated from our feelings or our bodies. Group psychotherapy began to help us communicate with others - thereby easing our sense of alienation further. Transpersonal or spiritual psychotherapies put us in touch with our 'Inner Selves' and with spiritual realities. But a further step is now necessary - we need to heal our alienation from the world itself. And so in response to this need, many people are turning to a study and practice of traditional ways, of earth-religions, to re-discover their sacred connection with the world around them. This latest step in the process of disalienation represents the leading edge in the consciousness-development movement that began to accelerate so dramatically from the 1960's onwards. The rediscovery of the power and relevance of the earth religions, and the sacred traditions of the land, has to a great extent been pioneered by psychology, through what can be loosely termed the human potential movement. Mainstream psychotherapy, however, has not taken this step, because it is caught in the belief that it is 'curing the outer world by making better people' as the Jungian psychologist James Hillman has expressed it. In *We've Had a Hundred Years of Psychotherapy and the World's Getting Worse* he goes on to suggest that 'therapy, in its crazy way, by emphasising the inner soul and ignoring the outer soul, supports the decline of the active world'.

Notwithstanding Hillman's opinion, psychotherapy does help us explore our experience of the pain of being in the world - of the difficulties and challenges which we face, and of the alienation we experience. The psychologist Rollo May had a sign in his waiting room that read: 'Either way it hurts.' In other words: if you ignore the problem it will hurt, if you face it, it will hurt.

This adage applies to the world-soul as it does to the individual soul. In relation to the central problem that faces us all, we must either take the path of unconsciousness or consciousness. The path of unconsciousness is the ostrich-path that refuses to face the problem, but which drives the despair and sense of powerlessness deeper. But it is a tempting path, for who among us can say we can truly face the pain of a world that is so damaged?

The path of consciousness requires an attempt to see what is. This first step needs no action, it simply requires seeing. We all know the experience of watching some terrible scene of suffering on the television. We look away, then when we think we can face it we turn back - looking through our fingers perhaps. Until again we must turn away. There is a progressive, or fractional, integration of awareness. This is the path of consciousness. The path of unconsciousness turns the television off, or switches channels.

This book is about a path of consciousness, about a way of seeing the world, but it is about a path of hope rather than despair, a path that leads from an initial acknowledgement of the woundedness of our world, to an experience of the wonder and unity of all life.

This path is an ancient one, and has been walked by many people since time began. Today it can be illuminated not only by ancient tradition but also by modern understanding.

Everyone must find their own locality.

Richard Jefferies

In the work of individual healing, of psychotherapy, our first step towards change is paradoxically to stop for a moment our attempt to change, and instead to accept who we are. We must learn first to stop trying to get away, and start trying instead simply to see, and accept.

Why are we trying to change, to 'get away'? Because what we experience is suffering - pain and ugliness, and a sense of not feeling at home in the world. To stop trying to escape from suffering seems a lunatic suggestion, until we discover that the gods seem to like paradox, and that as soon as we stop striving and start accepting, things start to change...

The Tump

The only place you can begin a journey from, is here.

The Tump

At Newgrange, that great belly-temple of the Goddess in Ireland, there are spiral patterns carved on the portal stone and in the inner chambers. At the Tump in Lewes the spiral is to be found, not carved in stone, but sculpted in the earth herself. A broad spiral path coils itself around the mound, starting in the North - place of darkness and beginnings - and finishing by opening out onto the broad flat summit of the mound.

Walking the spiral path today confronts us immediately with the central problem of living in the modern world. We find ourselves in a world that is ugly and damaged. The beginning of the path is hidden in the back yard of a large house that faces the main road and railway station. The only way we can tread the path today, without trespassing over private property, is by walking to the back of the Bowling Club hut that stands beside the Tump, negotiating rubble and rubbish, to stand almost at the path's beginning.

But once we have done this, we find ourselves facing a gateway that beckons us towards a different land - a land still to a great extent undamaged - still filled with primeval beauty. And most importantly for us today - filled with an ability to teach us.

What an odd thought for a modern mind to grasp! How can the land teach us - what can it have to say about the issues we struggle with individually and collectively?

Here we come to one of the key distinctions between what are known as the revealed religions and the natural, indigenous or earth-based religions.

'Revealed' religions are based upon the revelations of one or more people - such as Jesus, the Prophets, Mohammed, or the Buddha. Teachings that depend for their sole source of inspiration on the message of one or a few people (almost invariably male) include not only the major world religions, but also all guru-centred movements. The 'earth religions' - in complete contrast - teach that our prime source of learning and inspiration is the earth herself. Here there are no sacred books to kill or die for - no dogmas to defend or dispute: only Nature herself in all her grandeur and simplicity, to guide and inspire us.

But what, in practice, does this mean? At this stage in human development we cannot just cast aside the accumulated knowledge of centuries, and return to a simple rural life in which Nature will magically provide all the solutions to our desperate problems.

And yet our book-learning and our science has led us ever closer to the Wasteland.

What we need to discover is a way in which we can reconcile the necessity to learn from the earth with the need to build upon, rather than reject, the accumulated knowledge of centuries. A clue to the way in which we can achieve this reconciliation is provided for us by a consideration of the symbol of the Holy Grail.

In *Le Roi du Monde*, René Guénon remarks on the similarity between the word *grasale*, a grail or vessel, and *gradale*, a book. To find the Holy Grail we must unite primordial vision, our deepest sense of wonder at the natural world, with primordial tradition - with a study of the ancient wisdom tradition whose written manifestations span over two thousand years of human endeavour.

John Michell, in his book *Twelve Tribe Nations and the Science of Enchanting the Landscape*, clarifies this essential understanding of the significance of the Grail in this way: "The vessel [*grasale*] contains the inspiring potion which returns whoever drinks it to the state of primordial vision. The book [*gradale*] signifies the primordial tradition. These two things are inseparable in constituting the full meaning of the Grail, either one of them being ineffectual without the other....The first without the second provides a fleeting sensation of no lasting benefit; the second on its own is lifeless and without purpose."

Here we have a key which is both profound and utterly simple. A key which is commonsensical and inclusive. We are not called upon to reject the accumulated wisdom of our ancestors, and we are not called upon to reject the primal experience of being-in-the-world with all the awesome power and horror and beauty that this entails.

Those who have spent time at university will know of the extraordinary sense of lifelessness and loss of meaning which can sometimes haunt the libraries and corridors of those institutions which have lost all sense of the sacredness of life. Those who have spent time opening themselves through means natural or unnatural to the primordial visionary experience know of the fleeting nature of mystical or altered states of consciousness. Somehow for the Grail to be truly established in our hearts we must reject neither experience nor learning, but must unite both in a way that results in our coming to a full and meaning-filled knowledge of life, that is satisfying at every level of our being.

As the gateway at the beginning of the snake-path beckons, I am not called, therefore, to abandon my learning. Instead I am called to unite that learning with my experience of the land.

The Druid Tradition is first and foremost a tradition of the land. It is an earth-religion. It requires a listening to the earth. But it is also a wisdom tradition, and as such carries a heritage of written material. The tendency amongst students of the esoteric is to believe that people in the past had better conditions for development. The reality is that no better conditions have existed than at the present time. We have the potential to learn from far more material than was ever available to the Druid of ancient times. We have access not only to far more material regarding the primordial tradition, but this material is enormously enriched by studies from other branches of learning. Druids were doctors, judges, philosophers, astronomers, and educators as well as magicians and shamans. We know far more now about these subjects than the Druids of old. But we are lacking in something that they undoubtedly possessed to a greater degree. We may have more books, but they would have had a relationship with Nature that was markedly different from ours today.

Our quest, therefore, in following the Druid Path today is twofold. On the one hand we must find and organise the relevant written material - accessing the written heritage of our native tradition. But just as importantly, we must find a new relationship with Nature - so that she too can become our guide and teacher.

Even in this respect our task is not to attempt to return to a state of consciousness enjoyed by our ancestors or the Druid of old, but to find at our turn of the spiral of time what it means to be at one with the earth and sky - with the goddess of the land and the god of the clouds and thunder.

In being called by the Tump to begin a journey, I was being called to rediscover the primordial vision I had enjoyed as a child. But this time I was to seek the goddess not for a mother in whom I could forget myself, but as a teacher who could show me the way in which I could unite the knowledge I had accumulated as a student of Druidry with an experience of nature that would make that knowledge valuable and meaningful and relevant to the world in which I found myself.

The Gateway

Long is the journey
to the centre of the heart.

Nuinn

The journey began with a gateway - a natural gateway formed by a beech and yew tree. The ancient Druids understood gateways and all that they mean. Some scholars now say that proto-Druids built Stonehenge - and Stonehenge acts as a gateway for the solstice sunrises. Each stone circle has its gateway - its entrance place between two stones. Irish folklore is full of tales of people who disappear into the land of the Sidhe, the fairies, by accidentally, or deliberately, walking between two trees which act as a gateway into that other world.

Each of us is a living gateway between the inner and outer worlds: as the poet Novalis said, 'Visible and invisible, two worlds meet in man.' A tradition like Druidry teaches us how to walk through the gateway that separates everyday consciousness from an altered state of awareness that allows us to experience life in a deeper, more inner way.

Before we can do this we stand first at the Gateway and ask permission of the Spirits and Guardians of this sacred tradition if we may go forward. If our life-path is to take us elsewhere we find we never really enter into this world. Other interests absorb us, we follow a different way for a while or for a lifetime. But if the call is there, if we're meant to follow this path, we find ourselves drawn towards the stones, towards the trees that stand to either side of us.

And there we are at the threshold - as if waiting our birth. To the left is our mother, to the right our father. The crackling energy that passes between these two pillars fuses in our beings and we are propelled through and forward. At birth we tumble naked and tiny into this world, at death we tumble out into the Other World, perhaps finding our parents greeting us yet again - as they did at our physical birth. And so walking through the gateway with intent forms the first step on our journey. If we do this consciously we die and we are born - we change in some way - often in a subtle sense that only becomes apparent after some time.

Beginning this journey I touched the beech to my left and the yew to my right. The Yew - *Ioho* in Irish - is the tree of death and rebirth, a sacred tree of the Druids. On mainland Britain the Oak was the central tree of Druidry, but in Ireland it was the Yew. Recently it has been found that yews can live for at least 3,000 years - and this fact, combined with it being an evergreen, points to it as the tree of eternal life. And yet in the popular imagination it is a tree of death – partly because its leaves are poisonous (its Latin name *taxus* may be the origin of our word toxic) but mainly because it grows in churchyards. The mundane explanation for the favouring of yews near graves is that it kept animals out of the churchyards - both they and their owners knew of their danger. The esoteric explanation is that this represents the survival of a pagan knowledge that the Yew was the tree of rebirth and eternal life, and that it was therefore most fitting as a graveyard tree.

In the Druid tree-calendar, *Ioho* is placed at the time of Samhuinn (pronounced Sow-in). Samhuinn is the time of the death and rebirth of the Celtic year, in the three days between 31st October and 2nd November. At this time we honour the Ancestors, the Departed Ones, and prepare for a new cycle of the year. Later these three days were Christianised and became Hallowe'en, All Saints and All Souls days.

So what a perfect tree to find at the beginning of the journey! I touch the tree and ask that I may die to illusion, to all that is hindering and no longer necessary, so that I may enter a new cycle of joy and creativity and life everlasting.

To the left is the Beech - another sacred tree of the Druids, symbolising tradition, learning, wisdom, ancient knowledge, books. I lean against the grey skin-like bark, and look down at the beech nuts which still lie at the base of the tree. In old times these nuts, together with acorns, would provide food for pigs - totem animals of the Celts, sacred to the goddess Ceridwen. Beech is *Phagos* in Irish, *Fagus* in Latin, and is known as 'The Lady of the Woods' - native to Britain and a great deal of Europe from Spain to Norway, and as far east as the mountain forests of eastern Europe. In Britain it prefers the chalk of the Downlands, so here in Sussex it is a common tree.

Druids were sometimes known as piglets - and as such they fed on the food given by Phagos, the tree of Tradition, the Lady of the Woods. I bent down to eat an ancient knowledge nut. I found great resistance to identifying as a piglet, until I realised the genius in asking followers of a spiritual way to identify with such an animal. To take the piglet for one's totem requires humility - and humility is the first requirement as we walk through the Gateway.

Understanding that the quest involves uniting experience with the knowledge-tradition, the discovery of a beech and yew at the very beginning of the journey is a wonderful 'coincidence'. Experience comes when we allow ourselves to follow the voice of the Yew: to die and be reborn. Knowledge comes when we allow ourselves to be fed by the Beech - the accumulated wisdom of the past. Working with Druidry centres to such a degree on relating in a specific way to the past, to our history. And in doing this, we establish our roots and draw on our heritage, and we also secure our future. Hilaire Belloc said of a study of history:

'By the recovery of the Past, stuff and being are added to us; our lives which, lived in the present only, are a film or surface, take on body - are lifted into one dimension more. The soul is fed. Reverence and knowledge and security and the love of a good land - all these are increased or given by the pursuit of this kind of learning.'

As I lean against the tree of Ancient Knowledge, I feel the smooth beech bark on my skin and I ask that my soul be fed, that I might take on body, that I may learn from the past, that I may be lifted into one dimension more, that I may love a good land.

And I look around at the rubbish and the railway track and the road, and I realise that my hatred for this ugliness has made me hate my land. It has been hard for me to love the goddess we have made ugly through our wounding.

As I stand under the beech I understand that the solution to the problem of how we treat the earth lies not in denying the pain of the world, but somehow in including it - starting where we are: taking on board both the beauty and the ugliness of the world around us and of our own lives. This is difficult, and having understood this, I still found the road, rubble and railway ugly and would have preferred Shangri-La.

Can I step forward now to begin my journey? Yes.... and the first thing I must do is climb a fence and then depart from the snake-dragon path, because a wedge of this sacred hill has been dug out to accommodate a bowling green.

Rodney Castleden in *The Wilmington Giant* has called this assault on the Tump 'an astonishing act of vandalism'. Is it only in England that people can chop bits off sacred sites that may be thousands of years old without a moment's thought? Undoubtedly not, but there is a strong element of philistinism in the English character. And it is this disregard for our heritage that allows us to propose building over the Rose Theatre (which happened) or building a military museum next to Stonehenge (which didn't happen), or that allows us to damage or destroy - for example - in only the ten years between 1954 and 1964, 250 out of a total of 640 ancient monuments in one county alone (Wiltshire). These are just some examples - a whole book could be written about the behaviour of the one-dimensional, bulldozer-brained people who think nothing of ploughing up an ancient barrow to sow a few more square yards of barley, or of capitalising on Britain's most lucrative tourist attraction by displaying our splendid ability to effectively kill and maim people, regardless of the fact that this site happens to represent to the whole world our extraordinary spiritual heritage.

So now I must risk sprained ankles to avoid the chasm dug by the one-dimensional bowlers, to struggle up to the point where the snake path begins again.

Now the way is clear. The sun shines - the sky is a brilliant blue and the skylarks are swooping low over the flat land below. Looking ahead, the path is gorgeously green. The grass, uncut all winter, is about six inches high and fresh with dew. Seven feet wide it carries me up to the top, like a great green river. I could just lie on it, pink and naked like a new-born piglet, and be drawn upstream by the curling snake herself.

And so I turn round and round the Tump, curling in and up, till I find myself lying on the summit. And there I am spreadeagled on the belly of the Goddess, gazing up at the sky.

'Come, Sky God,' I hear her saying. Does she call to Taranis, the Thunder-god of the Druids who will fertilise her with one stroke of his lightning and the soaking rains of his life? Or does she call to the Dagda (literally 'The Good God') the great Father-God who will take his huge spoon and stir her cauldron till it brings forth an abundant life of flowers and fairies, animals, heroes and more gods and goddesses?

I must sleep here. Here on these sacred mounds we are at a place lifted up - close to the sky, close to earth. The two meet and mingle, make love, move together. And if we are quiet we can hear the earth breathe and sigh, and we can feel the pulse deep within.

Merlin's Enclosure - The Blessed Earth

The song still remains which names the land over which it sings.

Martin Heidegger

I had been lying on a feature of the landscape which can be found all over Britain. Sometimes called mounds, sometimes called mounts, toots or tumps, most are almost certainly artificial hills - built for a mysterious reason or reasons that we can only surmise from our viewpoint thousands of years later. They are important and powerful features of the landscape of Britain. But what do we mean by Britain? Ask any person in these islands and almost all will be at a loss to fully explain what territory is meant by the term Britain, as opposed to the United Kingdom or Great Britain, or the British Isles. And few will know the origin of the term itself.

When I was challenged at a workshop in America as to my racial identity, I felt a moment of panic. I felt uncomfortable being English, surrounded by so many of Irish descent. But then I remembered some of my ancestors were Scots, so who was I? An Irish participant then astonished us all by saying she felt ashamed being Irish, and I replied that I felt ashamed to be partly English, considering all we had done. But then I realised we were both being absurd: to be conscious of the injustices of our society, past or present, is one thing, to feel personal responsibility for our ancestors' (or indeed contemporaries') misdeeds quite another. It's time we stopped suffering guilt on behalf of other people – otherwise Germans are forever condemned to feel guilty because of the Nazis' behaviour, Russians because of Chechnya, and so the list goes on to include almost every nation.

I discovered that to call myself British, rather than English, was a more accurate description - for Britain traditionally includes the three countries of England, Wales and Scotland. Why is it sometimes called Great Britain? This is to distinguish it from Brittany, Lesser Britain - 'Lesser' because it was colonised by the British in the early centuries of the Common Era.

The island of Britain derived its title from the Romans, who gave to the titulary spirit of the island the name Britannia - perhaps a development from the name of an early conqueror Prydein, son of Aedd the Great. But before this time the island had had many names: Clas Merdin, Myrddin's Precinct or Enclosure, was its first name according to the Triads, the wisdom sayings of the Bards. Later, the Triads say, it was called the Island of Honey.

Caitlìn Matthews, in her book *Arthur & the Sovereignty of Britain*, points to an intriguing connection between Prydein and Prydwen, King Arthur's ship: "Prid, pridd or pryd may mean, variously, 'dear', 'earth' or 'beauty'. The suffix, wen, from gwen or gwyn, means 'white' or 'blessed', so that Prydwen might signify the 'White or Blessed Earth'."

Each land is of course blessed, and part of our work today is re-membering the sacredness of the earth - an earth that has been de-secrated. Part of this work involves discovering the inner sacred landscape that lies beneath the veneer of the modern industrial age.

This sacred landscape carries different names with different associations to the outer names with which we are familiar. The outer names of the three countries of Britain: England, Wales and Scotland, act as coverings to the powerful inner names of the three realms that make up Merlin's Enclosure: Logres, Cambria, and Alban (England, Wales and Scotland respectively).

Here in Logres today our land is perhaps more wounded than in the countries of Alban and Cambria. The South has been more prosperous, more populated, more built upon. There are more people-per-square-mile, more cars, more pylons here than in the wilder, more mountainous, more majestic terrains of Wales and Scotland.

But even so, we can still discern the sacredness of the landscape - in stone circle, holy well, terrestrial zodiac, ancient trackway, and sacred mound.

The most well-known of these mounds is Silbury Hill near the massive stone circle of Avebury in Wiltshire. When I speak of mounds, I am in this context being quite specific. I do not mean the mounds that are tumuli - round or long barrows. I mean instead, human-made, often quite steep-sided mounds with flat tops. These mounds are so important to an understanding of the sacred landscape that Alfred Watkins began his seminal book *The Old Straight Track*, with a study of them, although he included in the compass of his study mounds of all types, including tumuli.

Tumuli are burial mounds or initiation chambers or megalithic sweat lodges - places of darkness, of death-and-rebirth, of the embrace of the goddess; of sensory deprivation and of vision questing, of isolation and of communion with the Ancestors. They were of the long or round type: sometimes indicating a communal burial place in the long versions, an individual one in the rounded versions. But the key place in a tumulus is within it. The power exists within its womb-chamber.

Sacred mounds, which are sometimes called 'tumps', are different in purpose and character. The place of power is atop it. You can't enter it physically because you are not supposed to - there is no chamber or passageway to its heart. The summit often looks like a UFO launch-pad - it is unnaturally flat, whilst the sides seem unnaturally steep. Excavation proves them to be artificial, and traces of burials within them are seldom found.

These sacred mounds are not confined to Britain. I have seen them as far away as Peru, and as near as Holland. In Peru, near the shores of the world's highest lake, Titicaca, lies a strangely haunting site called Sillustani. There great towers were built to house the corpses of the dead - with open tops like huge furnaces that allowed the vultures to enter and perform their work. Beside these towers is a perfect stone circle - identical to a classic European megalithic circle, and a little way further off is a sacred lake, out of which rises a mound that looks like the identical twin of Silbury Hill.

In between the villages of Berg en Daal and Beek in Holland, just by the German border, two conical mounds rise out of the forest. With flat tops and steep sides they are clearly places of power, and their names indicate this too - they are called the Devil's Hills. Whenever something is called the Devil's this, that, or the other it's a sure indication that they were used by Pagans, and that power resides there. The incoming Christian Church rededicated them to the Devil to dissuade people from visiting them.

So conical hills with truncated tops that create a circular platform on the summit are not confined to Merlin's Enclosure. Even so there are a remarkable number of these hills to be found here, and Watkins gives photographs of four of them in his book: Hundred House Mount, Turret Tump, the Batch Twt, and Capler Camp.

The most famous of them, at Silbury, was excavated in 1968-9. The results disappointed many people - no burial chamber was found, no chieftain or king accompanied by grave-goods was disturbed by the archaeologists. But what they discovered was in reality far more exciting. Deep inside the great mound they found a small conical hill. Under this was found a radial pattern of ropes. The organic matter excavated from beneath the mound gave a radiocarbon date of 2145 BC (+/- 95 years). The remains of vegetation and trapped insects even suggested a particular time of year that the mound was raised - the last week of July or the first week of August.

Midway between these two weeks lies the time of Lughnasadh, the harvest festival which later became Christianised as Lammastide. In Scotland up until the 18th century Lammas towers were built to celebrate this festival. Conical mounds about eight feet high would be built of turves, and each community would build a tower in a conspicuous place, which served as a focal point for the Lammas celebrations. John Anderson, writing in 1792, said: "From the moment the foundations of the tower were laid it became an object of care and attention to the whole community."

The information obtained from the Silbury Hill excavation strongly suggests it was a hill built for the Lughnasadh celebrations - a giant harvest hill created by probably hundreds of people. And here in Lewes there is almost certainly another one.

If the Lewes Tump is a harvest hill, that explains the extraordinary sense of fecund power one gets looking at it, touching it, climbing it.

Here our ancestors would have climbed in celebration the snake-path towards the summit. There they would have looked down at the ripe fields and up at the sun blessing their land. To the south they would have seen the floodplain with its two islands stretching into the distance - a plain flanked by Swanborough Hill to the West and Itford Hill to the East...

The Spirit Of The Journey

[The Road] is the humblest and the most subtle, but, as I have said, the greatest and the most original of the spells which we inherit from the earliest pioneers of our race.

Hilaire Belloc.

Although the impulse to set off on a journey to discover the sacred landscape around me had come at the time of Alban Arthan, I was not ready to leave until the beginning of February - at the festival of Imbolc, Christianised as Candlemas.

Leaving the hill that morning was easy. Thanks to the rains of the previous day, the sky was clear, and I could almost hear the voice of the Tump saying - "Go, go - you will be back soon and I will always be waiting for you. I'm not going anywhere." So, with backpack and walking boots I walked fast, almost running, down the path, alongside the bowling green and past the ruins of the Benedictine Priory which stand beside the railway track which leads from Lewes to Brighton.

I paused for a moment by the ruins, to look once again at the few old walls that remain of this vast building whose church alone was once larger than Chichester Cathedral. This town, for some reason, has attracted an extraordinary amount of ecclesiastical establishments. The Priory was founded in 1077 by monks from Cluny, a prestigious Benedictine house in Burgundy, and later Cluniac houses, such as Reading Abbey, were subject to the Lewes Prior's authority. It was from the Priory that pilgrims would gather before setting out upon their pilgrimage to Santiago de Compostella. In 1190 the Archbishop of Canterbury refounded the monastery, which had been in existence since at least the 8th century, at adjacent Malling. There he also established a College for a Dean and six Prebendaries. At some time before 1241 the Franciscan Grey Friars had also established themselves in the area - this time just outside the east gate. By then the town and its suburbs already supported fourteen churches, and was home to the Court of the Archdeacon of Lewes - whose tasks amongst other things was to hear cases relating to slander and 'sexual ungodliness'.

Now all that remains of the great Priory are these few walls. The Franciscan Friars have gone, as has the Archdeacon – perhaps because we have at last found sexual godliness, and his services are no longer required. Gone too is the College at Malling, and of the fourteen churches of Lewes just nine remain to preach to their dwindling congregations. Gone too is the church of St Sepulchre, on Albion Street, which rumour suggests may have sheltered the Holy Grail. Whereas in the USA 86% of the adult population claims a religious affiliation, in Britain only 48% of the population does. Britain is considered a Christian country - yet statistics indicate that it is becoming increasingly secular: within forty years probably less than 0.5% of the population will attend church regularly.

But it is a Christian country in the sense that its collective psyche is steeped in Christian culture, even though most British people would not call themselves practising Christians. But it is also a Pagan country. Its collective psyche is rooted in its pre-Christian Pagan and Druidic past, even though most British people would never dream of calling themselves Pagans or Druids.

I walked on, through a tunnel that runs under the last vestige of the modern world that I would meet for a long time. The roar of traffic from the A27 faded behind me as I crossed the stile that led to the first of many footpaths.

And suddenly there she was just standing there - waiting for me: a young woman in her early twenties, perhaps, with long blonde hair and pale sea-grey eyes. Shimmering yet still, she stood looking directly at me. "I am Niwalen," she began, in a faint but crystalline voice, "my name means 'The White Track'- I am the goddess of the Road. I am the Spirit of the Journey."

She took my hand and pulled it towards the earth, so that I was forced to kneel down. As both our hands touched the earth a quiver of light travelled along the ground ahead of us so that I could see a line of silver light flowing across the field - far into the distance across the flat land and towards the horizon. "This is the White Track across the Blessed Earth - across Merlin's Enclosure," she told me. "Follow it and you follow your heart. Follow it and you will find what you have been seeking." I looked into her eyes, and then at her feet. There were the white trefoils - the white clover flowers that spring in the footsteps of the goddess of the Road, wherever she treads.

I was only ten minutes from my front door, two minutes from the main road - but already I was a thousand miles and years away from the grime and din of the town and its traffic.

I began to walk, and as I did so, she disappeared as fast as she had appeared...but from that moment I would always feel her presence as I walked the path that began in a gentle curve to lead me towards the village of Iford.

The sun was shining brightly and, as I walked towards one of the many rivulets that drain the Brookland basin, I felt the weight of years falling from me. I found myself laughing uncontrollably as I could feel - literally - inner psychic matter, stuff, weight, tumbling off my back and shoulders and down into the earth beneath me. The worry and concern, responsibility and care, engendered and nurtured for over forty years found a more solid home in the good hard earth below. Who could not worry for themselves and their children at this time? Worries galore had filled my life: I had worried when I was rich (the tax bills! the accountants' fees!) I had worried when I was poor (the tax bills! the food bills!) I had worried before each child had been born (will they be healthy?) I had worried after they had been born (will they stay healthy?) I had worried for the world, and worried for myself... but now these cares sloughed off me without any effort on my part. I had spent hours in psychotherapy analysing my concerns with a concerned person, and now they had gone - at least for the moment - and it seemed so natural I hardly gave it a thought. I just laughed and laughed until I saw a man walking towards me along the path.

Now that's a strange experience. To feel a goddess beside you is one thing. But to look up and find a single man walking towards you in open country is another thing entirely. In the city you are protected by buildings and other people on busy streets. But on a trackway it is different. You are forced to acknowledge each other - each is forced to sense whether the other is friend or foe. With a nod and a 'Good Morning' we pass - he making his way to town and me making my way towards another Gateway - a gateway in the hills.

I paused at a stile and looked around. Being on a floodplain surrounded by high Downs I felt as if I was in a chalice - a broad wide cup with a flat bottom teeming with life - with fish that swam in the many cuttings that drained the plain, and with birds that were celebrating the first stirrings of spring. A blackbird, a Druid-Dubh as he was called in the old days in Scotland, sang in the hawthorn beside the stile. Druid-Dubh means 'the Druid bird'. It is he who welcomes the company of Culhwch sent by King Arthur to perform thirty-nine tasks set by the giant Yspadadden Pencawr before Culhwch may obtain his sweetheart Olwen. And then I remembered - Olwen is another name for the goddess of the Track - Niwalen. And there she was again, standing by the stile with the blackbird on her shoulder.

"Remember, little piglet," she said, "that the Druid-Dubh is the first of the Oldest Animals. Ask of him a question - and await his answer." I closed my eyes to think of a question, but when I opened them she had gone. Only the blackbird remained - singing on the stile beside me. I bent down and looked into his eyes. They seemed so old, so sad "What has become of all the animals and plants who no longer grace our land?" I asked him - remembering that by the end of the century, in only seven years' time, we will probably have extinguished between one-half and one million plant and animal species.

The blackbird paused in his singing, looked directly into my eyes, and then began a song that rose and fell in a way that led me into a peculiar trance-state I had never experienced before. And there, in that state, I just knew his answer. He did not speak or tell me - his song simply took me there. And there was here only different. It was no other space, no other time. We were still in the Brookland basin, the sun still shone, the small white clouds still scuttered across the sky. But there were dragonfly and butterflies everywhere: chequered skipper, large blue and Adonis blue danced their way over flowers only my grandparents would have seen. Mother Shipton moths competed with pretty chalk carpet and dark brocade moths in the undergrowth of cowslips. Stone curlews, lapwings, hawks and falcons flew high and free in the sky above.

Then I understood! Just as modern man has the arrogance to believe his planet is the only one out of millions of planets to hold intelligent life, so we have the arrogance to believe that we perceive the only reality that can possibly exist. At some level, some inner, deeper, essential level, nothing can be destroyed. We can crush and break the forms but we can never destroy the essences of things. If the world were to be blown up by madmen in Washington, London, or Beijing tomorrow, I knew then that somehow somewhere none of the splendour of nature would be lost - it would continue to exist in the inner world until the time came for it to manifest outwardly again.

But then the rise and fall of the blackbird's song drew me back to my everyday state of consciousness, and as this happened a great despair overwhelmed me, and I looked into the blackbird's eyes and I knew why he looked so sad. This world, this everyday world exists too, and it is the only one of its kind. The essence of all that has lived here can never be destroyed and it will live forever in the inner world and perhaps on other planets and at other times, but here, now, it is unique and it can be destroyed and it is being destroyed. The world is mortal too, like us. And suddenly I felt like a child who finally realises that his parents will die one day... Suddenly the ground beneath you falls away and you are filled with a kind of dread. It doesn't matter that you are small and weak - you just need to know that your parents, your mother in particular, will be there for you to cling to for ever and ever. It's all very well saying that there will always be mothers - but you want this mother here, forever.

And we are the first generation to know this. To know that our Mother can die. Might die. For a child this realisation will, all things being well, lead to an increasing maturity. Let us hope that our understanding of our Mother Earth's mortality will lead us to a sober maturity rather than a nihilistic despair or an insane attempt to actually ensure her death. Psychoanalysts, after Freud, have been obsessed with our unconscious desire to kill our father (through the Oedipus complex). How strange it is that so few have observed the deeper, more sinister urge in the human heart – the desire to kill our mother.

Having shown me, in his trance-song, that Nature is both immortal and mortal, Druid-Dubh flies away, singing still and heading North.

But my way is taking me south - south towards Iford.

White Tracks - Sweet Tracks

There was an old woman lived under a hill,
And if she's not gone, she lives there still.

Traditional

Climbing over the stile, I walk along the track, marvelling still at how quickly the ugly signs of modern life have disappeared. The roads have now become invisible, and the only sign of human life is the occasional cottage in the distance, or if I turn around and look back, the town of Lewes itself. And it looks magnificent in the sun - the old houses clustering together beneath the castle that crowns the hill. The only eyesore is a massive modern office building rising incongruously to one side of this symmetrical gathering of buildings. And what an irony it is that this ugly disturbance to an otherwise beautiful scene should have been built to house the County Council - that body which ensures, among other things, that the planning laws are enforced so that no-one may raise a building that could be considered offensive - another 'astonishing act of vandalism'. Since this book was first published, Lewes residents have unsuccessfully lobbied to have the building demolished.

Something else strikes one forcibly about the splendid view of Lewes from this vantage point, and that is the prominence of the Tump. There it is: a large, distinct feature of the landscape - a major element in a consideration of Lewes as a whole. And yet in the town itself few people pay any attention to it. It is popularly believed that it is made up of the rubble excavated from the old salt flats - now called the Dripping Pan. Others believe it is a Calvary Hill constructed by the monks at the Priory - and hence its use today to raise a cross at Easter. But both explanations for the Tump are incorrect. The fact is that the Tump lies outside the Priory grounds and it is hardly likely that the monks would have trespassed to create this mound when they had plenty of land of their own. It is also far too substantial a hill to have been made as a Calvary - which need only be a small mound. The origin of this idea comes from a medieval Christian attempt to give a gloss of respectability to a pagan monument that was remarkably close to a Christian establishment.

As we look at the Tump from a distance, its similarities to Silbury Hill are striking. Rodney Castleden has enumerated these: both are artificial hills, both are made of chalk, both are turf-covered, both are conical with the apex of the cone absent, both have a circular platform at the summit, both have slopes at c.30°, both have ledges or ways below the summit, both have valley-floor sites with nearby wetlands, both have a base diameter/height ratio of 4:1.

Why, then, should they be so similar? We find the clue to this enigma when we consider Logres as a whole, at the time these sacred hills were constructed: around 5,000 years ago. They both formed part of a network of sacred sites that stretched right across the land. There are only two differences between Silbury Hill and the Tump. One difference is that Silbury has a single ledge running just beneath the summit platform, while the Tump has a snake-path. The other difference is that Silbury Hill is much larger:

Silbury is 130 feet high, the Tump 42 feet. The diameter of Silbury's base is 520 feet whereas the Tump's is only 170 feet. If they were both constructed as Lughnasadh harvest hills, then their size would have related to the size of their local communities. Silbury stood near the great complexes of Avebury and Stonehenge serving the numerous local megalithic communities whose alterations to the landscape are still to be seen throughout Wiltshire. The Tump served a smaller population. But what is common to both is that they were built at key points in the network of trackways that crossed the land.

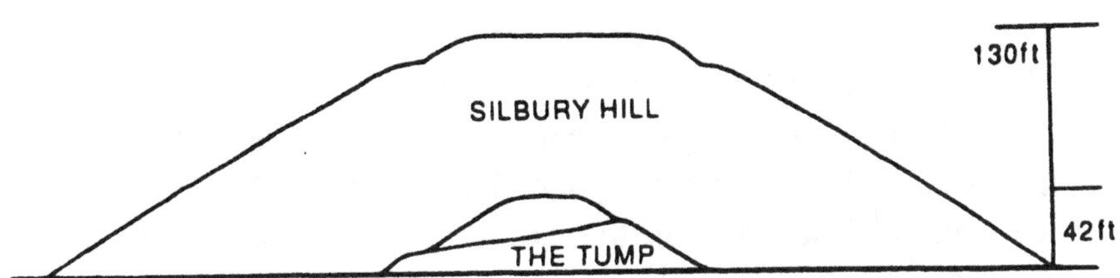

fig 1. Silbury and the Tump

To fully appreciate the tradition of Druidry, and its ancestral underpinnings in the ancient British tradition, we must learn about these trackways, for they represent one of the prime means through which we can connect to the ancient, but ever living, tradition. Hilaire Belloc said that the road represented 'the greatest and the most original of the spells which we inherit from the earliest pioneers of our race.' Just as fire evokes within us the appreciation of Spirit, and we feel drawn to a fireside as if by an implacable spell, so too does an ancient trackway evoke in us the spirit of journeying and the experience of both freedom and belonging to the earth.

Much attention has been given to the phenomenon of ley lines in recent years, but before we turn our minds to a consideration of how these trackways connect sites and how they might have been used for communication and geomancy, we need to look more simply, more directly, at their basic, their primeval power.

There is no better way to begin doing this, and to begin a study of Druidry, than to start walking the ancient tracks, and this is far easier than it may at first sound. After just one experience of such walking - in consciousness - we will have participated in an activity that has been carried out by our ancestors for almost half a million years. To fully appreciate all that this means, we need to understand not only the origin of these trackways, but our own origins too.

The first human beings were thought to have begun living here at least 450,000 years ago, and although great sheets of ice were to descend from the Arctic at various times, they never touched Southern England.

During the coldest times, our ancestors shared this land with mammoths, elks, bears, woolly rhinoceroses, reindeer and horses who roamed across the treeless tundra-steppe countryside. In the warmer periods, we shared great forests of birch and pine and open land with hippopotami, elephants, lions, spotted hyenas, bison and deer.

So we have occupied this land for about 450,000 years. For 423,000 of these years we lived in the open air - camping by rivers and lakes - wherever we had access to big game. Some traces of such camp sites have been found - such as the one bordering the shallow, reed-fringed lake at Caddington in Bedfordshire.

Flint was used to make tools, and life probably consisted

fig.2. Map of Britain showing the maximum extent of the ice sheets.

of small nomadic family groups following herds of animals from place to place, enriching their meat diet with wild plants and berries.

Then a veil of ignorance descends on our knowledge of our predecessors. For 10,000 years there seems to have been a break in human habitation here - although we may well never know what really happened. Then around 17,000 years ago humans reappeared, although different in kind. Before, up until the 10,000 years break, they had been Neanderthals. Now - from 15,000 BCE onwards - *Homo sapiens* was living here. The ice sheets finally retreated north from Scotland, and after six thousand more years, the tundra and steppe were replaced by forest.

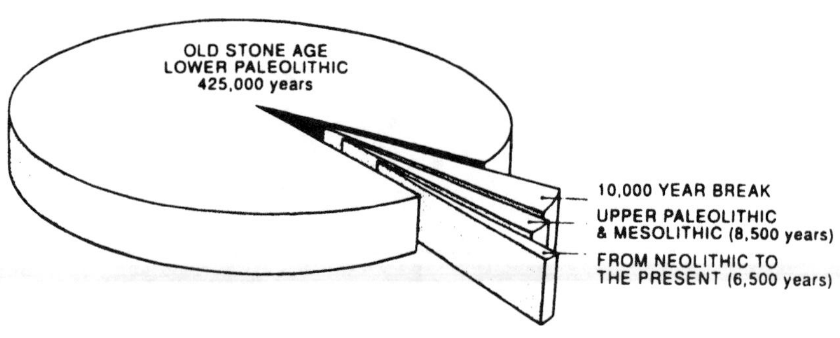

Fig 3. Time Scales

Whereas Neanderthal camped by rivers and lakes, *Homo Sapiens* preferred caves - ideally cave mouths where fires could be lit and windbreaks could be made from skins and branches. Such caves have been found in the Cheddar Gorge, at Wookey in Somerset, at Kent's Cavern in Devon, at Victoria Cave in Yorkshire and at Creswell Crags in

Derbyshire. We dressed in furs, and decorated ourselves with necklaces and bangles made from carved bones, shells and perforated animal teeth. We used flint to make scrapers, spear-heads and knives. And at Paviland Cave on the Gower Peninsula in Glamorgan, Wales, we see evidence of ritual activity: the corpse of a young man has been found buried with a covering of red ochre, and beside him lies a mammoth's skull, shells and an ivory bracelet. And most exciting of all - ivory rods, which could be the earliest examples of magic wands ever found.

At Robin Hood's cave in Derby a rib bone has been found, engraved with the image of the forequarters and head of a horse, and at Pin Hole cave in Derby a reindeer rib carved with a human figure has been found.

These are virtually the only known examples of the art of these times – evidence of cave paintings has now been found in Britain, but weather conditions have destroyed all but traces of these.

From the appearance of *Homo sapiens* in 15,000 BCE up until 8,500 BCE the soil was completely frozen except for the top yard during the summer. Only small stunted plants survived these harsh conditions - such as mosses, lichens and dwarf birch. No wonder Druids call the birch the Pioneer Tree, and allocate the number one to it numerologically. It is the tree of beginnings, of birth, of the first level of training in Druidry, and is the tree whose blessings we must invoke if we are to begin a new project.

And so this land was blessed first with the Tree of Beginnings. Then, around 8,500 BCE there was a sudden rise in temperature. The ground thawed and the birch could grow tall and spread its forests across the land. Pine joined the birch, and these then gave way to hazel and finally mixed forests of oak, elm and lime.

Meanwhile, the melting glaciers and ice sheets meant that the water level rose over 150 ft. Thousands of acres of land were lost beneath the sea, and as the weight of ice was lifted from the ground, the land rose up in places. The pine forests that made up the land to the east of Britain became submerged and formed instead the bottom of the North Sea. In Scotland and Northern Ireland new land rose from the waters to be colonised by plants, animals and humans. By 6,500 BCE we were separated from the continent by water which flowed up the English Channel. At first narrow and marshy, with tidal rivers flowing through them, the straits then became the sea we know today - although we should remember that even up until the end of the nineteenth century large areas of land were exposed in the Channel at low tide.

By this time, the Irish sea had already formed, and Merlin's Enclosure was indeed an enclosure - surrounded on all sides by water.

And here, standing near the southern coast of the Enclosure, I could almost see the inhabitants of this region in their dug-out canoes gliding silently across the Brookland Basin, heading towards the hill of Lugh in the distance.

By the time Britain became an island, around 6,500 BCE, the great monuments of Silbury Hill and the Tump would not yet have been built - nor the great and small stone circles that would, starting two thousand years later, begin to spread across the land.

But although the monuments were not yet in place, gradually, from about this time, the matrix out of which the monuments would grow began forming. Slowly, a network of paths was being formed as the inhabitants travelled between seasonal sites, sources of raw materials, and fording places of rivers.

Trackways would have existed in the Old Stone Age, but in most of Britain, each Ice Age would have erased these. In Southern England there is the possibility that trackways began to be permanently engraved on the landscape, although the dramatic changes in climate, vegetation, and animal and human populations would have led to much erasure and change. But by the mesolithic period, which spans the years from 8500 to 3500 BCE, the goddess Niwalen, Olwen of the White Track, had begun to change the focus of her work from establishing the trackways on the subtle levels of the land to their establishment at the dense physical level. Some of these trackways were originally made by animals, and were then followed by man. Others developed functionally - linking habitations with flint mines or water sources, for example. Still others linked one encampment with another - giving evidence of trade and communication.

Others became major routes, and the term highway comes precisely from one particular kind of trackway that is distinctive in England: the high ways, the ancient tracks that follow the ridges of high land. Plotting these ancient tracks on a map immediately shows us why the great sites of Silbury Hill, Avebury and Stonehenge were sited where they were: for they lie, broadly speaking, at the point of convergence of five of these great trackways.

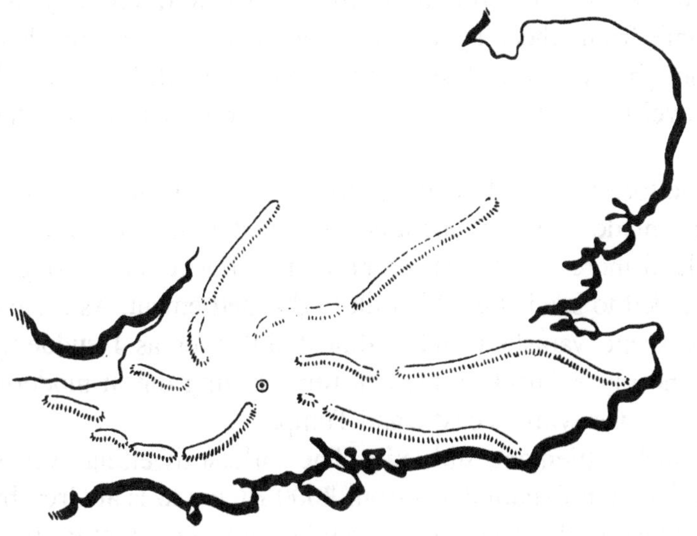

fig 4. Salisbury Plain & the Five Major Trackways

Most sightings of crop circles in Britain (estimated at 75% in 1990 by researcher Colin Andrews) occur within a triangle marked by Winchester, Warminster and Wantage. Combine this triangle with this map of the major ridgeways and one starts to understand why Stonehenge, Avebury and Silbury were built in this region.

Now I was standing on a minor trackway that would not have existed in mesolithic times, for this would have been under water most of the year. But I was heading for one of the most ancient and most important tracks - the South Downs Way, which in the east begins at Eastbourne and continues - even to this day - as far west as Winchester. In the old times one could have carried on directly to Stonehenge and Silbury.

As I looked back to Lewes in the sunlight, for a moment the Tump and castle vanished, the buildings disappeared too, and instead I saw just a hill, dappled in sunlight and with smoke curling from a settlement that was too distant for me to discern its details. Two canoes moved silently towards the hill. Looking to my left I saw where they had come from: there by the lakeside was a settlement close enough to observe. The canoes had clearly left from a small gravel beach, to either side of which grew willows trailing their branches in the water. Beyond these lay a birch and pine forest. Behind the beach there were conical houses like tipis made from timber frames wrapped with hides. Further inland there was a similar structure - but it was oblong. I decided to see if I could walk to this settlement. As I tried, the scene vanished and I almost fell over as I suddenly found myself back in present time, gazing out at modern-day Lewes with its castle and Tump.

Such settlements did exist. The earliest dwelling ever to be found in Britain dates from 8000 BCE and is at Greasby in Merseyside. There a rectangular tent-like structure with ridge poles probably 6 feet high has been excavated. The excavations at the Thatcham (in Berkshire) and the Star Carr (in Yorkshire) settlements has told us much about the lives of our mesolithic ancestors. At Star Carr it was found that the main animals hunted were red deer, roe deer, elk and wild oxen, but wild pig, water birds and fish were also included in their diet. The evidence shows the animals were selectively culled. A number of deer skulls with parts of the antlers still attached have been found. Since the insides had been hollowed out and holes had been cut into the frontlets, it seems likely that they were used as hunting masks or for ritual purposes. To this day in England we can watch the Abbot's Bromley Horn Dance in which the dancers perform with antlers on their heads. With the evidence of Star Carr we can conjecture that the dancers might well be acting out an ancient custom dating back 10,000 years.

At Star Carr beads of perforated amber have been found - reminding us of the Wiccan suggestion that female initiates wear an amber necklace in honour of the goddess. And in the Brighton museum we can see an amber chalice found in an ancient burial in nearby Hove.

So there we were, living in a way strongly reminiscent of the Native American, with tipi-like houses in small clans of four or five families, hunting and fishing, canoeing and tracking, with arrows and axes significant objects that were used both functionally and religiously. Flint arrowheads can still be found on the downland, and we find axeheads carved on one of the stones at Stonehenge amongst other places, and beneath the Sweet Track in the Glastonbury lowlands ritual axes have been found buried.

Having had one brief glimpse of life as it was, the lagoon turned from blue-green water back into grey-green grass. Lewes gazed back at me in a way that made me suddenly realise that she was a guardian-city. For she stands at a gateway. The gateway is formed by Swanborough Hill and Mount Caburn. Through the gateway we can work our way towards the heartland of Logres.

And the way we would approach this gateway - perhaps to take the guardian-city by storm, or perhaps to sneak round it by night - would be up the river Ouse: oozing and winding our way along the valley before curling round the Town and entering the Weald.

And just as I think that this would be the concern only of ancient times, I spot an old Second World War pill-box guarding the river. Even in modern times we have guarded these waterways leading to our heart.

The Songs of our Ancestors

The Songs of our ancestors are also
the Songs of our Children.

The track leads on and soon I find myself coming - not to tipis and deer-antlered men but to genteel houses - the sort which may well have deer antlers but which will be nailed firmly to shields hung from the wall, rather than tied to their owners' heads. Here at Iford the houses are beautiful, but they seem almost threatened by the great sweep of the Downs facing the Western side of the village. Up there on the high ridge is the South Downs Way, which in the old days would have led me to Stonehenge. From there I could have chosen one of the other great ridgeways to travel onwards to Scotland or the North of England, or into Wales or south-west into Cornwall.

Passing through Iford I carry on trekking until I soon reach another pretty English village - Rodmell. Here Virginia Woolf wrote her brilliant novels exploring the nature of time and experience, and here she finally chose to end the flow of her earthly life by drowning herself in the flow of the river nearby – a moment movingly depicted by Nicole Kidman in the film 'The Hours'.

The view from the churchyard in Rodmell is superb - but I find the church locked - something that in the old days would never have occurred, but now that one in five young men in Britain holds a criminal record, who can blame the vicar who wants to protect his church from vandals?

The track continues, to join up with the old South Downs Way at the worst possible place. Suddenly I'm back on the road again - with lorries thundering past reminding me that all is not idyllic.

The track I am joining has evolved over 10,000 years, perhaps more - its formation could have begun in the early paleolithic period up to 400,000 years ago. It is part of the landscape - one with it. Like a river this track and all the other ancient trackways of Britain flow through the land and are an organic part of it. The wooden trackways across the Glastonbury lowlands even looked like rivers. Our ancestors have left us a heritage of beauty, but we will leave in our turn metalled roads that lead everywhere but take us nowhere - for they have no soul.

Trying hard not to get angry with the cars as they roar past - for that car driver could be me on another day - I reach the tiny village of Southease, where I can turn off the main road and begin the descent through the village, and across the river. As I stand on the bridge looking back to Lewes - still bright in the sunshine - I imagine I am fording the river here. We're so used to bridges we give them no thought at all. I once walked from Port-au-Prince in Haiti to Jacmel - a town on the Southern coast. By the afternoon of the first day I was in wild country and came to a river. I can still remember the moment of utter astonishment when I realised I had no alternative but to swim across it. It had simply never occurred to my twenty-year-old self, raised in London, that such a thing might happen. I sat for a while staring at the river, before bundling my clothes into a bag and swimming to the other side.

Twenty years later, crossing this river is a wee bit easier, and as I walk by the willows and hawthorn that line the straight road that leads to Itford Hill, a voice says to me clearly this one phrase: 'The songs of our ancestors are also the songs of our children.' It is repeated three times. I stop to think about this. And everything suddenly swirls and whirls around and around me. And I hear again the great roar of Bronze age horns booming in the chambered passage of New Grange. And I hear again the chick-chick-chick sound of the bronze rattles, shaped in the form of bulls' testicles, that the proto-Druids shook as the trumpets blew. And I hear the high song of the Druidesses tumbling down into the sound-bowl of depth and darkness created by the low humming of the Druids. And then I hear just one lone voice - the voice of a woman singing in Irish or Welsh or English or Gaelic - I can't tell and it sounds so sad and yet so full of hope. And I know that to heal this Wasteland that we have made of our souls and land requires us to understand fully this sentence: 'The songs of our ancestors are also the songs of our children.' For if we believe in reincarnation, then our ancestors will and are returning as our children. And if they are not born on earth as children, but wait and watch in the Other World - then what sadness they must feel as they see us hurt and destroy each other and our home. Suddenly they are no longer back there - dead and gone - but all around us as babies and toddlers, children and adolescents - and of course as us - for we too are the Ancestors. There is no discontinuity in the line that stretches from the beginning to the end - which is perhaps another beginning.

And I know that I must walk on - to the real beginning of the ridgeway, up there on the hill. Crossing a railway track, I walk through a farmyard and then begin the climb. A few moments later I feel my old teacher beside me. I can't see him, but I feel him, and he begins to talk: 'Look down now at the farm,' he says, 'there have been farmers there for six thousand years. They began by building roundhuts - beautiful conical houses, with log walls and thatched roofs. Let's lie down and go there now!'

So I lay down in the sun on the slope of the hill and closed my eyes. I could feel the grass and chalk cool and firm beneath me - and the sun and the breeze on my face. And then I don't quite know what happened. The prosaic would say that I fell asleep, the mystic would say that I left my body and travelled back in time - my astral body finding its way along one of the tracks that exists in time rather than space.

Nuinn, my teacher, and I were wearing sandals and strange clothes of cloth, leather and fur. This felt comfortable enough as we walked slowly towards five roundhouses that stood before us on the slope of the hill. Smoke curled from the opening in the roof of the largest house. Children and dogs played beside it, and Nuinn turned to me to say, 'Touch nothing - they cannot see us, but they may feel us and we must not tamper with their lives.' We bent down to enter the largest house. Inside we found beds of grasses and furs around the walls. In the centre a fire was burning and a great cauldron hung above it. An old woman was preparing what looked like flat bread, and bunches of herbs hung drying from the roof beams. I counted these and saw there were nineteen of them. Nuinn saw me doing this and smiled. 'Remember our Imbolc ceremony in which we light nineteen candles? Now you know why!' And I thought back to the ceremony that we had celebrated only a few days before, in which the following was recited:

Nineteen candles are lit for Brigid
Your first candle lit is your sunrise birth: the flame of your house reaching Ceugant's brow
Second is the spark of your union with Bress, son of Elathan

Third is the pillar of fire, as you took the veil, rising high and clear
Fourth are brothers, Dagda the father, Broadb The Red, Medar, Ogma and Aenghus
Fifth is eternal life's spring: that sings your name, in crystal gaze
Sixth is the flame on your Altar, that never dies!
Seventh is the grove at Llandwynwn, on Mona's shore, where lovers tryst
Eighth is the strength of your oxen of Dil - Fea and Fernea, the red and the black
Ninth is the sigh of your breath, as new life grows from old, your bridge of truth
Tenth is a milk white cow, of redden ears, the Earth Mother's nectar, sweet
Eleventh is a girdle, that spans night and day, yet heals all and remains
Twelfth is a veil of truth, in a flowering thorn, your wearyall path
Thirteenth is for your son Ruardan, to be reborn
Fourteenth is the white light of the flowering word, born at sunrise - the molten sky
Fifteenth is the grove at Kildare, with solid oak and crystal spring
Sixteenth are shrines throughout Albion, in Church, Well and Wall
Seventeenth is your will, of black iron, forged in the determination of one thousand eyes
Eighteenth is a healing - the white dog at the portal, the chalice of your smile
Nineteenth is a clarsach which spells - hours, days and signs, all in a silver bough

Your last is your first, the beginning of the turning sea, the ending of the three
The dancing sun in the hearts of all! The candle that never dies!'

Just then a man entered the hut. I was startled. He seemed to look directly at us, but then he turned and talked to the old woman. He showed her something in his hand, and as he did this Nuinn quickly moved close to him and peered into his open palm. I didn't dare move. The old woman seemed to nod in approval, and he turned back to the doorway and began digging into the earth with a flat-ended stick. He then buried whatever he had in his hand - which seemed from where I stood to be a piece of chalk. As he covered it with earth, he murmured and chanted, and continued this whilst he trod the earth down with his foot. Finally, exchanging words once more with the old woman, he left the house. We left a moment later to visit the other houses.

It seemed as if the biggest house that we had just left was where everyone slept. The other houses were used for storing tools and food, for making pottery and for housing livestock. There was a fenced paddock to one side and further off we could see the terraced lynchets of the farm running up the side of the hill. The man we had seen earlier was now sowing along the lynchets. 'Barley,' said Nuinn as I looked at him questioningly. 'What was he burying in the doorway?' I asked. 'You know about doorways,' he said, 'they represent the meeting place of two worlds - the place of entry and exit between two places or two realms. The threshold is therefore a very important spot in a home. Remember the way a man is supposed to carry his bride over the threshold? That symbolises the support he will give her in all her moments of transition in their lives together. The piece of chalk that you saw him bury he had carved into the shape of a phallus, and he first asked for the old woman's blessing before placing it under the threshold. He did this to ensure the fertility of the farm, and to bring a blessing to their home. At the centre of the home is the cauldron, sacred to the goddess. At the threshold is the phallus, sacred to the god. This custom of placing a phallus at the doorway is one that can be traced from neolithic times right through to the fourteenth century - when phalli were carved on farm or church doorways.'

We started to walk up the hill towards an escarpment. There, at its crest was the cemetery - where, I was to discover later, a great funerary urn had been unearthed. As we reached the cemetry, Nuinn turned and looking directly at me, said 'We have all died and been buried in places like these. We have crossed the threshold into the Other World, into the Summerlands, into Hy Breasil. And we have come back, crossing the threshold again with the help of our parents, spiralling through the seed of the father and the egg of the mother to be born again in the cauldron of the womb. We come and we go, from one world to the next as the sun sets and rises again.' And then he was gone, and I woke up, or came to, with the sun on my face - lying there on the slope of Itford Hill that February morning at the close of the second millennium...

The Rainbow

Earth to air, rock into sun
earthskin flowered in mauve and yellow
lionpeaks and lionwalks skirted in growth:
windsculpture above the downland, and the fringe
of low thick trees with the streams deep-threading

Nuinn

Now I knew I was on the South Downs Way - for here at the top of the hill is a great wide way that runs west and east along the crest of the Downs. Having spent the morning down in the basin, sheltered from the wind and feeling warm despite it being February, I was now acutely aware of the season. The wind was blowing and the sun began to hide behind cloud. But the view was magnificent. To my right I could see the sea for the first time - silver-grey and striking in its flatness - as it lay contrasted behind the foreground of the Downs whose curves, like the great buttocks and thighs of an earth-goddess, dipped down to the sea at Newhaven far below to the South. And as if the land does indeed reveal the forms of the goddess, the river Ouse winds its way through open thighs to Lewes in the distance. And in the old times they knew that the land and the rivers were of the goddess - here the Ouse derives from the great mother-goddess Isis - Camden's *Britannia* tracing its origin as "Usa, or Ouse, in times past Isa".

I can still see the bright green tump - far away now, but seeming to shine with light, and it is as though the sea-god

Mannanan has swum the goddess' river to lay his seed where the water meets land. And the result is this glowing hill - pregnant with the god.

Up on the Downs and starting for the first landmark, Red Lion Pond, I can sense the presence of a hawk close by, even though I can't see him. I remember the piglet I began my journey with... he's gone now. He was my companion, my familiar of the plain, but here it is the hawk who flies high and sees all and whose spirit I can feel as I continue along the track.

This Downland landscape has such power. Now I understand why the occult writer Dion Fortune said that the chalk Downs were the best place to evoke the old gods, for they are *the* primeval landscape of southern England, and have been admired and written about by countless Englishmen and foreigners. John Aubrey (1626-1697) the father of the English Druid revival in the seventeenth century said of this landscape: "They are the most spacious plains in Europe, and the greatest remains that I can hear of the smooth primitive world when it lay all under water. And, to speak from the very bottom of my heart, methinks he is much more happy that at ease contemplates the universe as his own, and in it the sun and stars, the pleasing meadows, shades, groves, green banks, stately trees, flowing springs, and the wanton windings of a river, than he that with fire and sword disturbs the world, and measures his possessions by the waste that lies about him".

The chalk downlands were created from about 100 million to 65 million years ago, during the time the dinosaurs became extinct - before mammals, birds and flowering plants even existed. At this time the sea extended over most of what is now Britain. This sea was warm and filled with sponges and plankton. As the coccoliths, which are a part of the plankton, died and sank to the sea-bed, they created what we now know as chalk, combining with the sponges, and fish, sea-urchins, sea-lilies and ammonites, which we can now find fossilised in the chalk. This bed of chalk was then raised up out of the sea, like a great white whale of land comprising two thirds of England. And as though this event occurred only yesterday, as opposed to 40 million years ago, we find ourselves walking these 'broad backs against the sky', as Gilbert White called them, feeling literally the 'lifting up' of the land as if it were still happening - raising us closer to the gods by the minute.

And when we examine the geology of Logres we discover that the central node of the chalk downs was, and still is, Salisbury Plain. From it, outcrops run eastwards to the Hampshire Downs, and to the North and South Downs, westwards to the z-shaped Dorset Downs, and north-eastwards to the Marlborough Downs. So at the centre we find again the land of The Giants' Choir: Stonehenge.

And here on the South Downs I was on one of the long flailing spiral arms of the Giant - or rather of the goddess - for what could be more feminine in any landscape the world over than the soft sensuous curves of the Downs? But why are they called Downs when they are really Ups? Because the modern English word Down derives from the Old English and Celtic Dun, so beloved of Tolkien, and meaning a hill.

H.J.Massingham, making his home in the Downs, and feeling their likeness to the human body and their connection with our heritage, called them 'star-gazing shoulders... islanded in the past.'

And on this shoulder I was 500 feet up - not star-gazing but staring instead at a black cloud crying hard over the sea by Newhaven. Although not superstitious by nature, I sensed that I should not have looked at it - for it seemed to spot me observing its sorrow and decided to rush headlong towards me. I found myself walking faster, furious that I had forgotten to pack waterproofs. It seemed only minutes before the black cloud had caught up with me.

How absurd it was for me to be walking so fast - as if somehow I could reach a place of shelter on this open hilltop miles from any house or tree. The Druids practised divination by clouds - calling this art *neladoracht* - but it didn't take much art to divine the future from this cloud. Before I could determine exactly what black demon was determined to soak me I was pelted with hail and then with rain. I tried to pretend it was wonderful but it wasn't - I was drenched. But then as quickly as it had come it went - to find some other soul to pelt.

And then the miracle occurred.

As the cloud and its rain moved North, the sun came out and a vast rainbow spread across the landscape - stretching from Rodmell down by the Ouse where I had just been, far across to Firle in the east. And straight ahead, directly beneath and beyond the rainbow stood Lewes picked out in the sunlight.

I found myself shrieking and jumping up and down in my soaking trousers - what a gift that demon had given!

Something happens when you walk in this way. The exposure to the elements, the sense of height and openness, the increased oxygen intake and the effect of physical exertion all combine to produce a powerful feeling of elation. Throw in a rainbow and the effect is devastating!

If someone asks what Druid practice consists of, one way of answering is as follows: it involves working with the chalice and the blade. The chalice is the magic circle, the circle of stones or the grove of trees. The blade - sword or wand - is the Old Straight Track, the path, the journey. Our lives consist of rest and motion alternately, of being and doing as alternate states. In the Sacred Grove we find rest, we are calm, we are seated. We work our magic, we open ourselves to the breath of Awen, of inspiration, we find support in letting go of our obsession to do and to have. With the wand, the lance, the spear, the athame, the dagger, the sword, we move into the realm of Doing - we act in the world - we 'go forth', we journey. And in the Druid context we do this by literally journeying in the physical world. We throw a pack on our shoulders, a map in our pockets, and set forth on our own tradition of vision-questing - walking the old tracks.

And what we find when we begin questing can sometimes be disturbing.

One of the reasons for following a spiritual path, for taking that strange journey into the Self and into the world, is to discover the truth - the truth about ourselves and about Life. This is, in essence, the quest for enlightenment - for coming to an experience and a knowledge of 'What Is' as opposed to being ensnared by 'What Is Not' - illusion, *samsara*, untruth.

After the initial elation of setting off on the journey and discovering the wonders that are there for our exploration, we come to a point where we encounter demons and dragons. The sun is hidden behind clouds, it rains and the wind blows. The journey isn't that pleasant any more and we wonder why we began it.

From behind the clouds comes the dragon and we are faced with a choice. Do we fight it, or flee from it? If we fight it, we may well preserve the status quo, but at the cost of burying the power that the dragon represents. At an individual level, this may mean that we repress and foolishly believe we have conquered our sexuality, or our greed, or our lust for power. At a collective level we may repress an awareness of the dragon force of the earth currents that run through the land. If instead of supposedly fighting and mastering the dragon, we flee from it, it will continue to haunt the woods and the hill-tops or the sea - ready to harm us if we ever return there. A third approach - the approach of both the ancient wisdom traditions and of psychosynthesis - involves befriending the dragon.

One of the purposes of vision-questing is to do just this. In the Native American tradition you stay alone in a secluded place outdoors for at least three days. In the Tibetan tradition these quests occur for three day, three week, three month or three year periods. In the Christian tradition isolated retreats have also been part of spiritual practice. In Lewes we can still see the cell inhabited by an anchorite hermit. In the Druid Tradition, some groups call this practice 'Hero-Questing' for we are seeking the Hero Within. Sometimes these quests would have occurred in circumstances designed to create the effect of sensory deprivation, to which end trainee Bards would seal themselves in pitch black rooms and lie with a stone on their chest. The stone seems a strange prescription until we realise that the Bards were making use of a technique well known to modern psychology - that of creating one over-riding sensory input in order to block out all others. Nowadays we use 'white noise' fed in through headphones to the seeker in an isolation tank. Shamans use drumming partly for a similar purpose. After a while the brain becomes habituated to this one monotonous repetitive input and blocks even that out. A familiar example of habituation is that of a ticking clock - even though it may be loud, after a while we don't perceive the ticks any more: our brain 'hears them' but stops bothering to pass the message up to our consciousness until it changes.

And once the over-riding input is blocked out we are floating free - free of experience coming to us through our senses. What happens then is that experience comes to us in different ways - rising out of our subconscious as strange waking dreams, flooding in from our superconscious as powerful experiences of elation and inspiration. We find we can slip free of our physical bodies to explore a realm in which dragons can either be great sea-worms rising from the mud to haunt us, or jewel-encrusted mountain dragons guarding caves which hold for us those secrets which will change our lives forever.

But hero-questing or vision-questing can also be undertaken not in isolated places of retreat - in caves or dark bothies - but whilst walking the old dragon-paths as we journey from place to place. The outer journey then becomes a metaphor for the inner journey. The dragons that we find will then be either inner ones or outer ones, tied either to our souls or to the soul of the landscape we are exploring.

Lest we think, however, that we can befriend all dragons, we must beware - because there are dragons that are truly dangerous and are best left alone. We should not fall into the trap, so well laid by pop psychology, that seduces us with the idea that every repression can be lifted, every pain healed. It is an over-simplification to see evil as pain turned outwards as hatred. All we apparently need to do is fix the hurt and the evil will go away.... but 'fools rush in where angels fear to tread' and the wise know that the stories of dragons are there to teach us that the guardians of the treasures of the soul if approached naively or at the wrong time will wound and damage us. The individual and collective energies, complexes, call them what you will, that can be symbolised as dragons, are extremely powerful and can only be faced at the right time - and not before. And there are some dragons, demons perhaps rather than dragons, which are the result of evil thoughts and deeds and which only the gods can face without harm.

But what are and were dragons?

Up on this ridgeway I look north towards the Weald - a great expanse of lowland that lies beneath the Dun and which continues until the North Downs again rise up to provide another ridge of high ground. In the old days this was completely forested and much is still woodland. Thirty miles deep from north to south, from east to west it stretches across one hundred and twenty miles of countryside: from Romney Marsh in Kent to West Meon in Hampshire. At one time this massive forest was called the Waste of Ondred, and at another time the Forest of Anderida. The Venerable Bede described it in 731 as 'thick and inaccessible....a retreat for large herds of deer, wolves and wild boars.' And here, a little to the north-west just two miles from Horsham lived a dragon in the forest. In 1614 he was still alive - terrorising the neighbourhood. Described as being nine foot long with black scales on his back and red scales on his belly, the dragon 'rides away as fast as a man can run. He is of countenance very proud, and at the sight or hearing of men or cattle, will raise his neck upright and seem to listen and look about with great arrogance. There are likewise upon either side of him discovered, two great bunches so big as a large football, and (as some think) will in time grow to wings; but God, I hope, will (to defend the poor people in the neighbourhood) that he shall be destroyed before he grow so fledge.'

Some believe such creatures were exotic reptiles which had escaped from private menageries or were fictions put about by smugglers who needed to keep ordinary folk away from their hide-outs in the forest. The suggestion that dragon stories relate to a race memory of early man encountering dinosaurs cannot be correct, since sixty million years separate the final days of the dinosaurs from the appearance of humans on earth. Velikovsky believed that dragons were comets passing close to earth bringing disaster in their wake. Their bright heads and dark forked tails became the fire-breathing monsters of folk tales.

But to truly understand dragons and their relevance to the ancient traditions of this land, we need the help of Merlin.

Up here on the ridge overlooking the Waste of Ondred are two old dewponds - Red Lion Pond and White Lion Pond. Dewponds were probably being made up on the Downs as far back as Neolithic times, although some historians suggest they are a far more recent invention. A hollow would be dug out and lined with puddled clay and straw and then more clay - gradually building a waterproof lining to the hollow which would gather rainwater and the dew each morning. These dewponds have been maintained by local farmers to this day - although now, sadly, they tend to be lined with concrete. Why should one be called Red and the other White? We are reminded of the story of Merlin's boyhood when he and his mother were brought before King Vortigern, the king having been advised to sacrifice Merlin so that his blood could be smeared on the stones of a tower he was trying to build. Geoffrey of Monnmouth in his *Prophecies of Merlin*, continues the story in this way:

> *Merlin...approached the king and said to him 'For what reason am I and my mother introduced into your presence?' - 'My magicians,' answered Vortigern, 'advised me to seek out a man that had no father, with whose blood my building is to be sprinkled, in order to make it stand.' - 'Order your magicians,' said Merlin, 'to come before me, and I will convict them of a lie.' The king was surprised at his words, and presently ordered the magicians to come, and sit down before Merlin, who spoke to them after this manner: 'Because you are ignorant of what it is that hinders the foundation of the tower, you have recommended the shedding of my blood to cement it, as if that would presently make it stand. But tell me now, what is there under the foundation? For something there is that will not suffer it to stand.' The magicians at this began to be afraid, and made him no answer. Then said Merlin, who was also called Ambrose, 'I entreat your majesty would command your workmen to dig into the ground, and you will find a pond which causes the foundation to sink.' This accordingly was done, and presently they found a pond deep under ground, which had made it give way. Merlin after this went again to the magicians, and said, 'Tell me ye false sycophants, what is there under the pond.' But they were silent. Then said he again to the king, 'Command the pond to be drained, and at the bottom you will see two*

hollow stones, and in them two dragons asleep.' The king made no scruple of believing him, since he had found true what he said of the pond, and therefore ordered it to be drained: which done, he found as Merlin had said; and now was possessed with the greatest admiration of him. Nor were the rest that were present less amazed at his wisdom, thinking it to be no less than divine inspiration.

Accordingly, while Vortigern, King of the Britons, was yet seated upon the bank of the pool that had been drained, forth issued the two dragons, whereof the one was white and the other red. And when the one had drawn nigh unto the other, they grappled together in baleful combat and breathed forth fire as they panted. But presently the white dragon did prevail, and drave the red dragon unto the verge of the lake. But he, grieving to be thus driven forth, fell fiercely again upon the white one, and forced him to draw back. And whilst that they were fighting on this wise, the King bade Ambrosius Merlin declare what this battle of the dragons did portend.

Merlin then proceeds to utter a series of prophecies which begin with the overcoming of the red dragon (the British) by the white dragon (the Saxons) and continues by prophesying how the Boar of Cornwall (Arthur) will trample the Saxons. In an extraordinary sequence of powerful and often obscure images, Merlin predicts the history of Britain till the end of days, when the constellations of the Zodiac will cease to turn and the Goddess 'shall lie hidden within the closed gateways of her sea-beaten headland'. We shall return again to consider this prediction, but in the meanwhile why are the dragons white and red, and why are the dewponds here named after white and red lions?

The sacred animals of the inner world, like language, meet and merge with each other, producing fabulous beasts that portray features of the landscape both human and terrestrial.

The lions of heraldry and alchemy, that once in the flesh roamed this land, are images of the zodiacal sign of Leo, of the sun and of the element fire. Transformed into the winged lion, symbol of solar light and the morning, we can see its closeness to that other winged beast symbolising the element of fire - the dragon: as if the noble lion has united with the proto-dragon, the Worm - a creature famous in Britain in such places as Lambton and Linton, and recognised in the landscape at such places as Worm's Head in the Gower.

Another term for the dragon, common here in Sussex, is Wyvern. This term comes from the old French, *wivere* meaning both the adder and life. And suddenly one of the key themes of Druidry is illuminated for us. The Druid term for life-force is *nwyvre* or *nwyfre* - an old Welsh word meaning energy and vigour. In common with Eastern symbology, the snake is seen in Druidry as the prime symbol of the life-force that snakes both through the land and through us. If we want to understand this life-force it is not enough simply to discover it within ourselves - we need to discover it in the world around us too, for we are not separate from the earth, but a part of it. Here we find a contrast between the inward-turning methods of the east, and the outward-turning approach of the west - although both ways lead to the same point. *Wivere* derives from the old Gaulish *Wouivre*, meaning spirit, and this became *Vouivre* in certain parts of France, where the dragon became depicted as half-woman, half winged snake - a fitting symbol of the goddess' energy which snakes the land.

How beautiful it is that like Celtic knotwork both language and symbolic animals interweave to show us the relationship between ourselves and the land - between the dragon in our own body and the dragons of the earth. Inner and Outer, Self and Other, dance together as do the words *nwyvre* and *wyvern*: the Druid kundalini and the fire-breathing dragon, the kundalini of the earth goddess.

The purpose of both dragons, inner and outer, is the same. They convey the creative fire, the fertilising breath that brings life and abundance, both to the individual and to the land. For all sorts of reasons beyond our understanding, these dragons have been allowed to sleep. But we can imagine that in the old days they were awake, and it was the old sage, the Druid or Druidess, who knew how to direct and utilise this inner and outer fire, to creative ends. The quest for personal fertility - of ideas, of children, of song and music - and of earthly fertility in abundant crops, seemed as one in ancient days, and need to be united by us again as we try to extricate ourselves from the wasteland we have created within and around us.

And it is in the two colours of white and red that we find the clue to this fertility we need to rediscover: for white and red symbolise male and female, sperm and blood, moon and sun. Still to this day in somewhere as far away as Bulgaria, an old territory of the Celts, everyone will be seen wearing small pom-poms of white and red in March, in conscious recognition of the coming Spring, and in unconscious recognition of the Spring Equinox on 21/22 March and of the need to unite the two principles to create an abundant life.

The Ordeal

Draca sceal on hlæwe, frod, frætwum wlanc.
(The dragon shall be in the tumulus, old, rich in treasures.)

Beowulf

After White Lion Pond I entered a new phase of the journey. In a nutshell I would say that it was no longer enjoyable. My clothes were wet, the wind was blowing, the sun was now hidden, and both sky and land seemed great rolling masses of monotonous grey. Somehow I had stumbled into a black and white movie, complete with giant studio fan pointing my way. To cap it all it was lunchtime and through some monstrous oversight I had brought no food with me.

All along the track there are tumuli, and just beyond the Males Burgh Tumulus the track meets a small road running from the isolated Blackcap Farm to the village of Firle, lying at the foot of the Downs. It was here, at this crossroad, that I met the Devil. He looked ordinary enough, wearing a Barbour jacket, wellington boots and a scarf, but although he fooled me at first, in the end I knew he was the Devil.

He was munching a sandwich, and as I approached him - with every intention of simply nodding at him and carrying on - he said "Hungry?" "Yes I am!" I replied, believing for a moment he was just a friendly local man. "There's a good pub down in Firle," he said, "fabulous food, Harvey's Ale, a good fire. That's the place to go." "Yes I know...but if I walk down there," I said, gesturing to the village 500 feet below, "and have the kind of meal I'm seeing in my head, and a pint of Harvey's, I'll never get back up here." "Well why are you here anyway? What are you doing? Look at you - you're soaking! Go down there and sit by the fire and get warm!"

For the life of me I couldn't think why I was up here: something about walking old tracks, taking a journey that was both inner and outer, something about gateways - it was all very vague.

"You don't know what you're doing, do you?" He laughed, thinking he'd got me, but at that point his pride at having almost made a kill had the better of him - he shifted position and a great scaly red and black tail flopped out of his jacket and fell on the ground behind him.

"I'm walking this Way because I choose to walk it!" I shouted, and picking up a piece of flint from the ground I threw it at him.

I then started running along the track towards Firle Beacon - not daring to even turn round. Running a mile or so uphill after you've been walking all morning and are wet and hungry is no mean thing, and by the time I reached the Beacon I had had enough. I lay down on the Beacon's tumulus and would gladly have allowed myself to be carried away for roasting by the fire in Firle.

But there was no sign of the Devil. Instead I found myself sitting up and gazing at the view across the Waste of Ondred from this vantage point. Here I was 711 feet above the sea, and the monochromatic landscape was slowly changing to become, not brightly coloured, but subtly shaded in pale pastel. As the clouds broke, here and there the sun picked out isolated features of the landscape - the clustered buildings of Bopeep farm to the east, Decoy Pond and the tiny Firle Tower to the west.

It was a fabulous tapestry of delicate colours and as I looked I realised that it was a tapestry woven not only by Space but also by Time. Down on the plain I could see features of our modern-day world: the railway track running from Lewes to Eastbourne, Arlington Reservoir shining like a great lake, and here and there the sight of a road. But here also was the past in the present: to the west Firle Place, home once to some of my distant ancestors, and then directly below the Beacon, Charleston, the house frequented by the writers and intellectuals of the Bloomsbury Group. To the east, there was the village of Berwick which hosts one of the most beautiful small churches in the county. St Michael and All Angels at Berwick is almost certainly built astride a barrow and close by a second one, and it possesses two unique features. Firstly the interior has been painted by Virginia Woolf's sister, Vanessa Bell, her son Quentin Bell, and Duncan Grant - an artist who had been raised with his cousins Lytton Strachey, the biographer, and James Strachey, the translator of Freud. He lived with the Bells at Charleston until his death in 1978 at the age of 93 - having held long friendships with both Leonard and Virginia Woolf, Maynard Keynes, E.M.Forster and others. They began decorating the church in 1942 and their paintings show Christ in the downland landscape, echoing the words of William Blake when he asked: 'And did those feet in ancient time, walk upon England's mountains green? And did the Countenance Divine shine forth amongst those clouded hills?' Blake was referring to the legend that the young Jesus was brought to Britain by his uncle Joseph of Arimathea when he came here as a merchant, whereas Duncan Grant and the Bells have depicted Christ's birth by Mount Caburn beside Lewes.

The second unique feature of this church is that you can sit within it, and gaze not only upon downland scenery depicted on the walls, but also upon the real thing, rolling beneath the sky as you gaze out through clear glass to the surrounding countryside. The original stained glass was blown out during the war and mercifully it was not replaced. Most churches lock us away from the outside world - but here we can maintain our contact with the land. Outside we can walk up on to the old barrow and look around at the graveyard and church, and feel that here, at least, we are not witnesses to the result of a foreign religion that has usurped a power spot of our native tradition. Here the transition from barrow-site to church and graveyard feels organic and natural. Some Pagans feel angry about the way Christianity has taken control of sacred sites and changed the old ways by turning the eight Pagan celebrations of the year into apparently Christian ones. Whether we feel these take-overs were unjust or evolutionary varies according to our reading of history and our assessment of the benefits accrued or the damage done. But however we feel about Christianity's appropriation of our sacred times and places, the fact remains that it has occurred, and as more and more people awaken to the riches of our pre-Christian heritage, the challenge for us now can be expressed in this way: 'How can we reconnect to these sacred times and places, in a way that honours both our pre-Christian and our Christian heritage?' However, some of us may not be able to honour all of our collective spiritual inheritance: some may only be able to respect and venerate either the Christian or the Pagan, but not both.

Here at Berwick there seems to be no conflict between the old ways and the newer one, and this is partly due to the clear glass of the windows and the downland paintings. But conflict between the Old Religion and the incoming one there has been and conflict there is still - in some places.

Thinking of conflict I find myself back on the barrow on Firle Beacon, musing over my encounter with the Devil. I'm starting to feel guilty about throwing a stone at him - after all, maybe he was right - it is very cold up here. And then I remember the legend attached to this barrow.

A long time ago there were two giants, one who lived here on the Beacon and the other who lived four miles away across the Cuckmere Valley on Windover Hill. Being a giant is not easy - you need huge amounts of food, you upset people when you go for a stroll, and few people understand you. It is not surprising then, that giants occasionally become bad-tempered. The barrow that I am sitting on was once the home of the Firle giant and one day he quarrelled with his nearest giant-neighbour who lived by the Hunter's Burgh barrow across the valley there. They picked up huge boulders and hurled them at each other. The craters left from this Battle of the Boulders can still be seen - misguided archaeologists believe them to be hollows left by ancient flint mines and quarries - but we know better. In the end, the Firle giant took his hammer and flung it at the Windover giant, striking him on the head and killing him in an instant. Such was the impact he made as he fell to the ground on the side of Windover Hill, that we can still see today the outline of his body - carefully picked out in white blocks for us by the Sussex Archaeological Trust - close by the village of Wilmington.

It seems that throwing stones at people you don't like is highly commendable - even if they are not giants or the devil, and are simply humble Pagans intent on stealing your possessions. The story I am thinking about concerns St.Wilfrid who came to convert Sussex Pagans to Christianity in the 7th century. Christianity had not yet taken root in this part of Logres even seven centuries after Christ, because Sussex was strangely isolated by the great forest of Anderida, the Waste of Ondred, which separated it from the rest of Southern England. In the year 666 Wilfrid was sailing from France to England, when he found his boat beached on the Sussex coast. Rodney Castleden suggests this might have been on the Pevensey Levels a few miles east of Wilmington. Eddius Stephanus, Wilfrid's chaplain and choirmaster tells the tale:

'As they were sailing from Gaul over the English sea with Wilfrith, the bishop of blessed memory, the monks singing and chanting God's praise in chorus, a fearful storm arose amid the sea and, as with the disciples of Jesus on the Sea of Galilee, the winds were contrary. For, a great gale blowing from the south-east, the swelling waves threw them on the unknown coast of the South Saxons; the sea left the ship and men, retreating from the land leaving the shore uncovered, retired into the depths of the abyss.

And the heathen coming with a great army intended to take the ship, to divide the spoil of money, to take captives and to put to the sword those who resisted. To them our great bishop spoke gently and peacably, offering much money, wishing to redeem their souls. But they with stern and cruel hearts like Pharaoh would not let the people of the Lord go, saying proudly that all the sea threw on the land became as much as theirs as their own property.

And the idolatrous chief priest of the heathen, standing on a lofty mound, strove like Balaam to curse the people of God and to bind their hands by his magic arts. Then one of the bishop's companions hurled a stone blessed by all the people of God, which struck the cursing magician in the forehead and pierced his brain, whom an unexpected death surprised, as it did Goliath, falling back a corpse'.

A battle ensued between Pagans and Christians, in which five of Wilfred's men were lost. The tide came in, their ship was hastily refloated and made for safe harbour in Sandwich. What is impressive is the down-to-earth pragmatism of the Christians: no turning the other cheek, and no qualms about 'offering much money, wishing to redeem their souls.' But I wonder if Wilfrid had hesitated before undertaking such a journey in a year ruled as it was by the number of the Beast in the Book of Revelations - 666?

So there are precedents for stone-throwing, from the days of David and Goliath through to St Wilfrid's exploits. I'll stop feeling guilty.

There is another legend attached to this high place of Firle Beacon which says that within the hill is buried a silver coffin - and within that coffin is a hoard of treasure. On Mount Caburn, across the valley and to the North-West, it is also said that a silver coffin is buried - but within that coffin the treasure is not a hoard of gold coins but a golden knight. Both these legends remind me of a single mystery - that the way to the sun is via the moon, the way to the masculine is via the feminine: we must find the silver before we find the gold. This means that, at a collective and individual level, we must open first to the feminine, to the Goddess, before we can come to know the true nature of masculine power. Our world is dominated by the masculine, but it is a maleness that is in reality emasculated - and because at a spiritual level it is impotent, it is dangerous and has produced the Wasteland that we see around us. Someone has coined the phrase 'the tyranny of the weak': we think that strength is dangerous when in reality it is weakness which poses the real threat. There is nothing more dangerous than a weak man: look at Hitler - a pathetic weak man who wreaked untold destruction.

Time to move on! Feeling desperately hungry I begin the long walk to Alfriston - where I know, if I am lucky, I can get a meal without deviating from the track. The wind is still blowing fiercely, so much so that it is hard to look around. I walk the broad track looking down and ahead of me. I can almost see the carts and the men, women and children - their clothes gathered about them - walking the track ahead of me. This was indeed a High Way and the traces of their journeys from encampment to ritual centre, to ford and to market, are still here in the Aether waiting to be sensed by those who are gifted with the art of seeing and hearing along the old Time Tracks.

It began to rain, not in the brief sharp way it had rained before the rainbow had appeared, but in that continuous way with each raindrop seeming to contain twice as much water as the drops of a brief shower. This part of the journey seemed to last forever. The Way became ugly - all was grey and brown. Chalky clay clogged my boots and the only comfort I could draw on was my knowledge that the Ordeal is always an important part of any journey. As long as we stay in our familiar world we remain comfortable, but in the end we vegetate, or worse still rot. As soon as we start to stretch ourselves, to try out new ways of being and acting, we enter a zone of slight discomfort, which is exciting nonetheless. And at the extreme of this zone of stretching and slight discomfort we come to the next zone: of risk. Entering this territory we enter a world in which we can become uncomfortable in a very real sense. If we push ourselves too far we are hurt, either emotionally, psychically or physically. But if we can push ourselves just enough to break through to another level of being we can gain experiences of real consciousness expansion and ultimately character development and spiritual and psychological growth. This is why spiritual teachers recommend - when the time is right - undertaking an ordeal. And this is why initiations contain an element of the ordeal in them also.

Our major initiations do not take place in temples or even in stone circles. For most of us in the West they take place in bed. Our most powerful initiations are the great Rites of Passage - being born, dying, making love for the first time - and for most of us these occur on the white sheets of a bed. And all these Initiations are also Ordeals. What greater ordeal could there be than to be born or to die! And so it is that in our spiritual and psychological development we are provided with opportunities to undergo ordeals: in our life-path we can choose to leave jobs, leave countries, leave home, leave spouses, and all of these catapult us into new situations that are full of stress and yet which provide us with tremendous opportunities for change and growth.

Every spiritual system generates ordeal experiences for its followers: in one Native American tradition, for example, there is the Sun-dance where the dancers are hooked through the flesh of their pectorals to long cords which connect them to a tree erected like a Maypole in the centre of the circle. In the major world religions there are disciplines of fasting and pilgrimage. But something strange and perverted can creep into the ordeal-disciplines of the patriarchal religions, with their focus on penitence and self-mortification.

Undertaking specific ordeals in order to stretch one's physical, spiritual and psychological boundaries is different from engaging in sacrifice. Christianity is centred on the concept of sacrifice, and it is refreshing to read in the Manifesto of the Fellowship of Isis in Ireland, where Nuinn and I stayed, and which is one of the largest Goddess centred movements that also has a Druidic Rite, that: 'The Fellowship reverences all manifestations of Life. The Rites exclude any form of sacrifice, whether actual or symbolic. Nature is revered and conserved. The Fellowship believes in the promotion of Love, Beauty and Happiness. No encouragement is given to asceticism.'

So it is not asceticism, self-mortification, penitence, or sacrifice that we are being asked to undergo when we follow the way of the earth religions: instead it is a pushing of ourselves beyond our everyday limits to discover our true potentials. Walking the old tracks provides us with the perfect opportunity to do this: normally we might take a one or two mile walk perhaps on a Sunday morning. Instead we can try a five, ten or fifteen mile walk. If we plan the route well we can always chicken out and call a friend to come and pick us up, or dive into a local inn. But if we persevere we discover that we get a 'second wind' and then a 'third wind', and so on. We discover for ourselves the truth that we are more than we think we are.

And this is what happened to me on the track between Firle Beacon and Alfriston. I was tired and drenched. I wanted to give up the whole enterprise there and then. If a bus had miraculously driven past I would have hailed it and climbed on board. To negotiate the Downs it would have had to be a huge vehicle with enormous tyres, driven by the Firle Giant. As I boarded the bus I would have found myself nodding good day to my fellow passengers: the Devil, still munching his sandwiches, St.Wilfrid's men nursing their wounds, Virginia Woolf gazing out of the bus windows, daydreaming of rivers and the sea. But no such bus was in sight. Suddenly the rain turned to hail. I looked to my left and saw the hail bouncing off a newly ploughed field. In this one brief moment everything changed. The beauty of the whiteness of the chalk in the turned earth and the whiteness of the bouncing hail, told me I could carry on and I knew again that it was important to do just that.

I was into my third wind, taking great strides through the mud and rain. I passed a couple trying to ease on waterproof trousers and was glad I hadn't brought mine – the couple was just as soaked and were simply wasting time. It seemed only moments before I found myself in Alfriston, almost staggering down the steep lane that abruptly becomes sedate a street which houses the newer buildings of the village. It was three in the afternoon. Ten years ago there would have been no way of getting a meal in an English village at such a time, but now there was just a chance. It was then that I remembered the signs that hang in so many restaurants, tea-rooms and pubs in this part of the world: "NO WALKERS!"

I felt enormous and wild. My boots were covered in mud, my clothes were soaked, my hair was dripping. The day's deep breathing of downland air made me feel about nine foot tall as I stood examining the menu at the Tudor House. I spotted a table just by the door... and there was no waiter in sight. Now was my chance... if I could just get my boots tucked under the tablecloth before one appeared. I walked in trying to look nonchalant. It felt as if I was the Firle Giant crazed with the exhilaration of just having killed my opponent, trying to look cool as I sloped into a local bar. The restaurant was filled with a funeral party - no doubt mourning the death of the Giant's victim. A sudden hush descended as they stared at me, quickly looking away and resuming their conversations as I returned their stares. The waiter was charming, he smiled at me as if saying 'I know you've got filthy walking boots tucked under this table, but I don't care' and took my order.

As I sat back and awaited the food, I almost fainted. Suddenly the effects of the ordeal came flooding over me - I hadn't been on such a long walk since my twenties, and years of poring over a desk and computer had taken its toll. I thought about calling my wife from a payphone and having her pick me up after the meal. She could bring some dry clothes - yes! But no... I had to finish this first part of the journey - I had to get to that second gateway, I had to reach the Firle Giant's victim.

I had to reach the Long Man.

and when I looked at him I knew
that I knew him
and had always known him
when time was never.

Nunn

Just as King Vortigern was unable to build his tower because each night the stone walls which had been carefully built during the day were scattered by invisible forces, so the church builders at Alfriston had a similar problem. Every morning the builders found that the stones had been uprooted, whirled in the air and flung on to an ancient burial mound nearby. One day a wise man noticed that four oxen were lying on this mound with their rumps touching - forming an equal-armed cross. Accordingly the site of the church was transferred to the mound, and a cruciform building was raised on the site.

Having visited this old church, I walked beside the Cuckmere river, crossed by a footbridge and at Plonk Barn took a brief detour to visit the smallest church in England. Here again was a Christian church built on a pagan site, but whereas Alfriston and Berwick churches were built on mounds, this church has almost certainly been built in the very centre of a Druid Grove. The hurricane of 1987 and other storms have sadly destroyed many of the trees encircling the church, but it is still possible to sense the sacredness of the place. It was S.F.Annett, in an article for the 'Sussex County Magazine' in 1932, who first suggested that here at Lullington we may well have one of the rare survivals of a *nemeton* - a Celtic sacred grove.

From the church I retraced my steps, and crossing a broad sloping field, which gave fine views of Alfriston falling away to the west and Windover Hill looming to the east, I joined again the South Downs Way.

Crossing the minor road that runs from the hamlet of Lullington Court to the village of Wilmington, I began the ascent of Windover Hill. By now the afternoon was drawing to a close and I could sense just the beginnings of a darkening in the sky. I passed by a huge bunker-like structure wedged into the hillside. On the map it is marked as a reservoir - but going up to its huge metal doors and banging on them produced a booming dull echo as if they simply barred the way to a large room. This, combined with the fact that an aerial stands on its roof, suggests that it is one of those places that MP's or town councillors would rush to in the event of nuclear war. Tom Graves in *Needles of Stone Revisited* discusses the relationship between the ley network and the microwave system of communication that has been established throughout Britain for communication in the event of a breakdown in the normal electrical system through war. He came to the conclusion that at least some of the microwave towers were 'built on or very near to node-points in the natural energy-matrix.'

Dismissing images of a post-nuclear race sired by politicians and civil servants slowly emerging from their bunkers to scenes of utter devastation, I continued up the hill, to find myself standing on Hunter's Burgh - a long barrow which Rodney Castleden has suggested represents the phallus of the Long Man who lies below sans cock. Although he gives much reason to his argument, it still seems an odd idea that somehow the phallus has winged its way up here to lie above his head, rather than staying between his legs where it belongs. Barrows are not masculine phallic symbols, they are feminine: places of death and rebirth - literally tombs and symbolically wombs. We, with our linear separative consciousness, resist seeing the connection between the joyous birth of a baby and the tragedy of death. To combine the two images in one would be too much for most people to bear - as it would be to combine images of people having intercourse with images of babies being born or children playing. But our ancestors were almost undoubtedly steeped in a consciousness of the cyclicity of life - of the intimate relationship between life-processes: between birth and death, intercourse and procreation. One of the grossest mistakes of early anthropologists was to believe that 'primitive' peoples saw no connection between copulation and pregnancy - when almost universally the earliest manifestations of religion focussed on these mysteries.

The fact that a chambered tomb could be used for both burial and initiation strikes many people as odd, if not impossible. And yet what could be more appropriate? The songs of our ancestors are also the songs of our children - there is no discontinuity: we are born, we die, we are born again. This is why churches and graveyards are built together. Our culture which denies death would far prefer graveyards to be tucked away at the edges of towns so that when visiting a church we were not reminded of death....and this of course happens with many new and urban churches - but none of them has that extraordinarily tranquil timeless quality that we find in a church complete with ancient graveyard and yew trees. And this atmosphere of peace that pervades such a churchyard and church comes precisely from the fact that the line is not broken: people are christened, married and buried there. Here at any rate the Church wisely continued the tradition of the Pagans who in like manner revered the total life cycle.

Walking down from the barrow I found myself at last facing the Long Man - although like the Hanged Man of the Tarot deck he was upside down to me. He truly is vast - 227 feet tall - the second largest representation of the human figure in the world, second only to the Giant of Atacama in northern Chile, who stands 393 feet tall.

The giant's location is very particular. He has been drawn in a natural amphitheatre of the Downs, which means that from many angles he is obscured from view. Walking the South Downs Way over Windover Hill, you do not see him. If you are too far to the west or east of the amphitheatre you will also never see him. It is only when he is approached from the north that you come upon him gazing out at the northern darkness, and across the fields of Avronelle. This wonderfully evocative name is found in The Domesday Survey of 1086. In Sussex, the land was generally apportioned in 'hundreds' of between twelve and twenty square miles, but here for some reason the Hundred of Avronelle formed a separate unit of only five square miles, including within its borders the Long Man and Wilmington Priory.

Avronelle is reminiscent of the name 'Aurenelle', meaning Lady of the Dawn or Dawn Goddess, and some believe that the Long Man is an image of the Lady Avronelle's husband, Wildenhelm (Wilmington), who – once she died – stood holding his staff and her staff open to create a gateway between the two worlds, so that he could visit his beloved in the Otherworld.

Deviating from the South Downs Way you can gaze down at the Long Man from above his head, but although an old stile exists which gives access to the giant, too many walkers have trailed across him and have caused erosion. So if you want to appreciate him the right way up you must double-back towards the bunker-reservoir and follow the track which leads finally to a dewpond and a small ridged hill below and towards the righthand side of the Giant. This ridged hill, although possibly created from the debris of the adjacent chalk-pit, feels significant from a ceremonial point of view. None of the literature on the Long Man seems to make any reference to it, except Marian Green in *A Harvest of Festivals* who compares it to a similar hill below the giant chalk figure of a horse at Uffington. So unlike a conventional representation of a horse is this figure, that some have suggested it is really a dragon. This makes sense, since the hill beneath it is called Dragon Hill, and a local legend maintains that it was on this hill that St.George slew the dragon.

Looking up at the Long Man one is filled with admiration for those who originally carved his form into the hillside. They have created a vast and timeless work of art in the landscape. It is an interesting comment on our modern society that when we engage in landscape art it is almost invariably transient, reflecting our obsession with form rather than content: an American artist specialises in wrapping whole mountains in plastic, for example.

One of the most extraordinary things about the Long Man is that he has been created with a deliberate distortion that makes him appear normally proportioned when viewed from the surrounding countryside. If you took a plane and flew over him, you would discover that he has been drawn with exactly the right degree of distortion, so that when viewed from the ground this creates the effect of the giant actually standing up, rather than lying on the ground.

And in the failing light I looked around this ancient site and thought I saw dim figures circling in ceremony the small hill beneath the giant. The concrete dew-pond with its overhanging thorn tree became the sacred pool that received the *nwyfre* of the god towering before it. I noticed that the sheep tracks that cross the giant do so, mysteriously, at his crown, throat, solar plexus and base chakras, and that the outline formed by the chalk in the adjacent overgrown chalk-pit itself looks uncannily like a giant dancing man. This disused chalk-pit and lime-kiln becomes just another symbol of the way we vandalise these sacred places - that particular piece of burrowing having occurred between 1750 and 1850.

I felt a strange sadness creeping over me, and a confusion. I had begun, in the morning, with great joy, walking through the gateway of yew and beech. And here I found myself facing another great Gateway - formed here by the two long staves that the Giant holds to either side of him.

But I didn't know what this meant, I didn't know what to do, and I simply felt sad. Putting this down to fatigue and the waning of the day, I walked to the village of Wilmington. Passing the Benedictine Priory, I entered the churchyard of St.Mary and St.Peter. There beside the entrance to the church stands a massive yew, so vast and so old it is supported by thick poles and chains which hold together two huge trunks which flow like wide rivers of red and brown wood towards the crown. The church is nearly a thousand years old, but this tree is even older. Seeded perhaps two thousand years ago it would have been a large tree at the time the foundation stones were laid - now as it emerges from the ground its circumference is 23 feet. In the churchyard were the first snowdrops of the year, their white heads having appeared just in time for the season of Imbolc.

As I walked in the churchyard, all of a sudden I noticed a gateway ahead of me: two younger yews, but still large, formed a natural archway amongst the grass and tombstones. 'Aha!' I thought, 'here's another gateway I must step through.' But as I walked towards it, I was filled with an overwhelming sense that this was one gateway I should not enter, one threshold I must not cross. Those of us born in the post-war generation, who have been exposed to the whirlwind which has catapulted our psychic development through the flower-power, guru, human potential, new-age and now shamanic waves of experience can easily fall prey to the 'Ooh! This is new - let's try this' mentality which crosses threshold after threshold only to find something is still missing, still not right, or worse still that we are damaged, more lost than ever. Previous generations were fettered by the taboos of respect and restraint, whereas we discovered that change occurred when we were disrespectful and lacked restraint. But the time has come when we can learn to act with respect when it is appropriate, but also at times with a disregard for absurd or unreasonable restrictions on our experience. Respect becomes a recognition of the subtle and sacred, restraint becomes an acknowledgement that power evolves and works through limitation rather than despite it.

The gateway before me became awesome - a gateway to the Other World - a gateway I could not cross while I treasured my life here in This World.

Sitting on the grass, I thought of the Long Man behind me. He too stands at a threshold, guarding the gates to the Underworld, to the Otherworld. I walked back to the Priory and beyond it, to sit on a fence that allowed me to gaze again at the god.

And then the obvious cascaded into my awareness... illuminating my sadness and opening me to a new drama - a new story. Winston Churchill once said 'Men stumble over the truth from time to time, but most pick themselves up and hurry off as if nothing happened.' The secret is to just look - and in just looking we discover what we were looking for. And here just looking at the Long Man the most obvious was no longer hidden from me, for HERE WAS A GOD WITH NO COCK! Here was a man with no manhood. Here was a massive figure of power and potency with no organ of generation.

And that was the sadness that I felt in this place, for here is a man disenfranchised, a man rendered impotent, a man castrated. The other great hill-giant of Logres, at Cerne Abbas in Dorset suffers no such indignity - he stands with both oak-leaf club and phallus raised.

As I sat gazing at the impotent giant I felt my mentor Nuinn beside me again: "You remember the chalk phallus of Itford Farm?" "Of course," I replied. "Our ancestors revered life and revered in particular the means whereby life came into being. Nothing is more magical or more beautiful than the act of man and woman coming together to make love or conceive a child. Phallus and vulva and woman's belly were all considered sacred, for through them spirit entered the world and the cycle of life was perpetuated. This god has lost his phallus and he has lost his mate."

"What do you mean?" I asked, puzzled by his last remark.

"In the old days, not only a god was carved into the landscape, but also a goddess. Over there to the south, beyond Windover Hill, lies Hindover Hill. And there on its flank was the Long Man's companion - a great white goddess carved out of the Downs. The god's phallus was tall, like the Cerne Abbas giant's, and on festival days bowls of water would be ritually gathered from the pond at his feet and carried the two and a half miles across the fields to the goddess, whilst chants and prayers for the blessing and fertility of the land were sung."

"That's extraordinary! Does anyone know about this goddess? Or are you just making it up?"

"Not at all. Memory of her lingers still - T.C.Lethbridge, an old friend of mine, was told by a shepherd when he was a boy that the Long Man once had a companion, and that the two of them were known as Adam and Eve. Records from further back - the 1860's - show that folk in these parts remember such a figure on Hindover Hill."

Before I could speak, Nuinn began again:

"The fact that he has lost both his cock and his mate is profoundly significant. Why do you think so much of our beautiful world is being destroyed?"

"I don't know... greed and stupidity I suppose."

"Yes, partly, but it's not as simple as that. Our world is run by men now, as it has been for some time, but it is run by men who are in reality impotent. They seem to be potent, and have all the trappings of power - but it is a destructive power that they possess, not a creative power. Real creative power is the treasure that is guarded by the dragon. Men have got nowhere near this true power. They strut outside the dragon's lair in shining armour and wave their swords for the photographers, but none of them dares engage the dragon."

"What on earth do you mean - I'm completely lost," I said.

"When we started to believe that our bodies and souls were separate, and that our bodies were dirty, we began the process of the glorification of mind and science and the desecration of the earth. If our bodies were vile, so too was the body of our home - the earth. We exploited the earth and its plants and animals as we exploited women - who have always been closer to the natural, the instinctual. The chalice of the land became separated from the sword of the will and the intellect, and the sword became a weapon of destruction. The Goddess was forced to hide, as we hunted her down in our repression of women and the Feminine principle. We and our earth are in pain because we have denied Her for too long. The power of the land has retreated into the caves and hills and is guarded now by the dragons which we too tried to kill. The earth has become a wasteland because our swords have sought not union but conquest, and in an extraordinary vicious cycle, the more we have denied Her, the more She has hidden, and the more She hides the more we rage because deep down we seek not the conquest of her but union with her."

"Now I understand why man seems in a peculiar way to want to destroy the earth."

"Exactly. We know about that strange urge to destroy

the father, that Freud discovered and named the Oedipus complex. But the deeper layer of destructiveness that is only now about to be recognised is our collective urge to destroy our mother - the earth herself. She has been denied to us for so long, that we - as her children - are trying to tear her apart in our desperation to return to her embrace.

"Man like a wild beast now roams the wasteland of his making - his phallus wild with rage for the Goddess who is denied him. He plunges his weapon to the right and left of him, slaying and maiming with a lust for destruction that makes the blessing of his creative organ a curse that ravages the earth. His seeds, destined to populate the earth with beings, plants and creatures now weigh so heavily within his grain sacks that they beget monsters and demons who in their turn rape and destroy their mother and brothers and sisters. They have become not Oedipus, the father-slayer, but Orestes, the slayer of the Mother.

"Only those men who are mad act overtly with their creative staff of life turned to the purposes of destruction and hatred by their failure to unite with their opposite. They are the rapists, the sadists, the sexual offenders of our world. For most men the failure to achieve union with the Feminine and the destructiveness that this engenders is transferred from the genital to the cortical level. The pain of separateness, the pain of not being held, travels like a saddened and toxic impulse through the nervous system, paralysing the heart as it travels towards the brain. There, in the clothing of genius and might, they use this 'higher' organ to penetrate the veil and mystery of matter. The two cerebral hemispheres drawing their impulse from the two lower and smaller spheres of the testes, act together to finally tear apart every possible secret so that they, triumphant, can say: "I know. I have known this woman, Matter. I now have power over her. I can control the elements, travel to other stars, change the course of destiny. I have triumphed." But the triumph is bitter for them because they still stand alone. Just as the weaker sex is in fact the stronger because her strength is hidden and secret within her body, and the man is in fact weaker because more vulnerable, because that most delicate part of him is externalised, so the loneliness of being externalised still haunts mankind. Standing on the body of Matter-Mater he is still not united. But there is worse to come. The Mother is not dead. In penetrating to the secret of her construction, in splitting and tearing that apart, he has violated her inner sanctum and she will be avenged."

Suddenly I saw that haunting image of Robert Oppenheimer's face after the first atomic bomb had been dropped. The enormity of the discovery of how to split the atom had only then struck him: 'I am become death, the shatterer of worlds,' he had said, quoting the *Bhagavad Gita*.

I looked into Nuinn's face and then out towards the Long Man.

And there walking towards us along the path was a woman, draped in tattered black clothes, crying and wailing. A shudder ran through me to my stomach - I was filled with an awful feeling of dread. As she came closer I saw that in one hand she was holding what seemed to be a miniature forest, and in the other a miniature city.

"Look at her!" shouted Nuinn in a voice that was filled with anger and pain. "She is the Goddess who has been denied. She is the soul of every one of us who watches the world destroyed before our very eyes."

She came to stand directly in front of us. By now her wailing and crying were making me shake with anguish. Tears streamed down my face as I saw in one hand the tiny perfect forest, and in the other a minute walled city.

The words of Merlin's prophecies came flooding back to me:

'Also a damsel shall be sent from the city of the forest of Canute, to administer a cure. Once she has practised her oracular arts, she shall dry up the noxious fountains by breathing upon them. Afterwards, as soon as she shall refresh herself with the wholesome liquor, she shall bear in her right hand the wood of Caledon, and in her left the buttressed forts of London. Wherever she shall go, she shall make sulphurous steps, which shall smoke with a double flame. That smoke shall rouse up the Ruteni, and shall make food for the inhabitants of the deep sea. Tears of compassion will overflow her eyes, and she shall fill the island with dreadful cries.'

Who was this woman, and why had she come to stand before us?

I looked up at her face. Returning my gaze she began to speak: "Why, O man, have you betrayed your childhood? Why have you stolen it, corrupted it, denied it, made it less than it could have been? Why have you betrayed our world? Why have you ordered the killings, made the bombs, polluted the air, denied its beauty, tried to break it?"

I fell to the ground, weeping and shaking uncontrollably. "I had no choice," I found myself saying, "I was looking for my mother. At first I thought I could find her by running wildly here and there. But she never came. I then went very still and felt I would die. But inside the volcano was beginning. I resolved to tear the world apart to find her and be with her again." I was astonished at what I had said - I didn't even fully understand my own words. I stood up and faced her now, and as I looked into her eyes I no longer saw fury and accusation, but instead a clarity of expression that seemed tinged with the pain of separation yet filled with a yearning for union and burning with love. She said, "You have looked for me so long I was frightened you would destroy me in your searching. You paraded armies before me, not to terrify, but to impress me. You sent rockets to the stars and built huge buildings just for me. But we never met. I was told to hide. I have been told to hide no longer, or you will destroy this world in your search. I stand here waiting for you to approach."

I stepped towards her.

The Green Man

The hedges of quick are thick with may blossom
As the dancers advance on the leaf-covered King:
'It's off with my head,' says the Green Man,
'It's off with my head,' says he.

William Anderson

I had set off on my journey early one Tuesday morning in February, and had walked just fifteen miles or so from the Tump to the Long Man, arriving there at about five in the afternoon for the rendezvous with my wife. It had been just a day's walk over the Downs, but I felt as if I had travelled a thousand miles in space and thousands of years in time.

Of all the things that had happened on the journey, the last moments at Wilmington had been the strangest, the most disorienting and the most powerful. Over the coming days, as I thought about what had happened, I realised that I had been addressed by the goddess not as me, Philip, but as spokesman, as representative of man in general. I, in my turn, as I had replied to her, had spoken not from my personality, but from some other place - from some collective voice of the male soul perhaps.

I spent the following days writing down my memories of the journey, and as I came to recount this last episode by the Long Man, I realised that there was still one thing I didn't understand. Nuinn had said "The fact that the god has lost both his cock and his mate is profoundly significant." I had then seen how the mother-goddess had been forced to hide, and how the loss of Eve - the Hindover goddess - was a demonstration in the very landscape here of this loss of the feminine, but I couldn't yet understand the significance of the loss of the phallus.

I decided to do some research on the two great hill gods of Britain: the one at Cerne Abbas in Dorset so clearly in possession of his manhood, and the other at Wilmington so clearly dispossessed.

The Cerne Abbas Giant stands 180 feet high, and brandishes an oak-leaf shaped club in his right hand. His erection is 30 feet long and it was a common practice for barren women to sit on this - hoping for a cure. It was also believed that a cure for infertility could be obtained by making love on the giant - almost certainly on the phallus also. Such behaviour is easy to understand - it is instinctive. One time when I was at the Long Man, I and other walkers watched as a group of young people climbed over the fence, ignoring the sign that asks visitors to prevent erosion by not walking on the giant. As they marched towards the figure's head, a girl in the group separated from her friends and ran to his groin - lying with legs akimbo where the cock would have been.

Above the Cerne Abbas Giant there is a square earthwork, known as the Frying Pan. There a firwood Maypole was erected each year at Beltane, and the giant's phallus from being two-dimensional became three-dimensional and could be danced around in celebration and in hope for a fertile year ahead.

The Revd de St Croix recorded that in 1772 as well as the carving of the Cerne Giant, there were also to be found between his feet three letters surmounted by three numbers. If these did exist, they have long since disappeared, but on some aerial photographs traces of such figures still seem to haunt the ground. In the thirteenth century, Walter of Coventry wrote that the giant was called Helith and William Stukeley confirmed in the eighteenth century that this was his name in local tradition. Stuart Piggott suggests a connection between Helith and the name of a wild hunter, appearing in medieval French legend as Helequin or Hierlekin, and in England as Helethkin and Herle. Helequin later became Harlequin, and Herle is highly suggestive of Herne - who is also a hunter. There may well be a link with Helios, greek for Sun, and Hercules the sun god, with whom the Cerne Abbas giant has often been identified. Add to this information the location of the giant at Cerne with its association with Cernunnos, and we have a clear image of the archetypal male solar god.

Just as the Long Man in local legend was a giant whose outline was formed by his dying body, so too in Dorset it is said that the Cerne Giant was pinned down and killed by villagers as he lay sleeping after a huge meal of dozens of sheep. But others say he is not dead, and that each night he drinks from a nearby stream, occasionally pausing to eat a virgin. This must have given the local girls a perfect reason to lose their virginity as soon as they could.

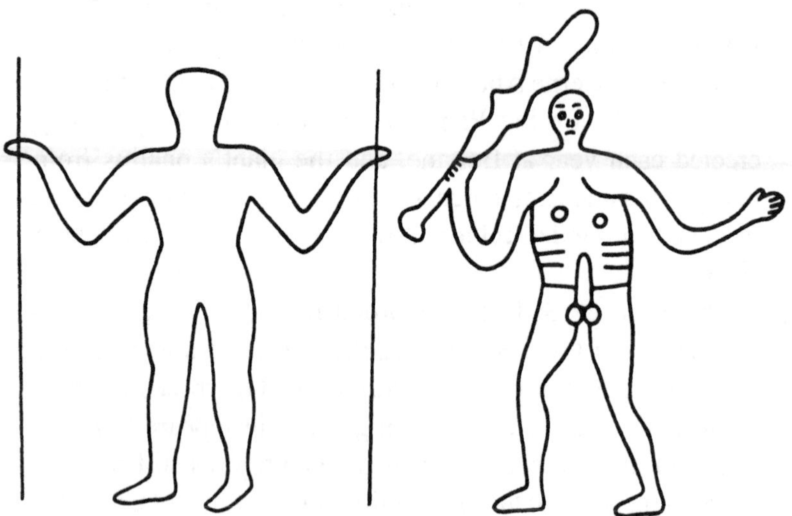

fig 5. The Long Man and the Cerne Abbas giant

The Long Man is taller than the Cerne Abbas Giant - standing 227 feet tall as against his brother giant's height of 180feet. To give an idea of the size of both of these figures, we just need to know that the colossal seated pharaohs at Abu Simbel are only 67 feet high, and that the statue of Liberty is only two-thirds the height of the Long Man. Whereas the Cerne Giant is rampant and full of movement, the Long Man is by contrast still and tranquil and evokes an entirely different response from the viewer. The twin weapons of club and phallus have somehow transmuted themselves into staves. These poles that the giant holds parallel to each other have been interpreted by some as measuring rods. One is 235 feet long, the other 232 feet. The shorter stave comes remarkably close to marking the long side of the standard Roman unit of land: the *jugerum*, which measured 232.2 t by 116.1. But this may well be coincidental, particularly since the measurements are of the restored staves, which may not necessarily match precisely the length of the original ones. Alfred Watkins believed that the Long Man was the 'dodman': a prehistoric surveyor, carrying the two sighting rods he needed to develop or survey the old straight track system.

The most convincing and satisfying theory that explains the existence of these two staves has been given by Rodney Castleden. To fully appreciate his argument we must travel along the South Downs Way and beyond - from the Giant of Wilmington to the Giants' Choir or the Giants' Dance that lies on Salisbury Plain: Stonehenge.

The key orientation at Stonehenge is towards the midsummer sunrise. This is why the Summer Solstice, of all the ceremonial times, draws the biggest crowds there, for Stonehenge seems 'made' for the Summer Solstice celebration. The midsummer sunrise is marked by the famous Heel Stone (a corruption of *heol* - the sun) which lies outside the circular ditch, or henge, that surrounds the stone circle.

A puzzle for students of Stonehenge had been that the Heel Stone did not accurately mark the pre-2000 BCE midsummer sunrise. But in 1980 excavations revealed the socket of a lost stone that once stood beside the Heel Stone. And the puzzle was solved: the sunrise was seen through the gateway marked by these two stones, not over the top of the Heel Stone as had previously been supposed.

The sun-god strode through the stone gateway into the cauldron of trilithons - into the womb and matrix of the earth-temple.

The archaeologist Aubrey Burl, amongst others, believes that the community which built Stonehenge lived at Durrington Walls - only two miles away to the east. An area of about 30 acres, surrounded by a bank and ditch, housed this community who lived and worked in great circular wooden buildings - rotundas. The largest of the rotundas to have been excavated by archaeologists was found to have been 127 feet in diameter, with a pitched conical roof and a central courtyard section left open to the sky. The doorway faced south-east, the direction of the midwinter sunrise. Two huge post-holes have been discovered which show that two pylons, taller than any of the posts supporting the roof, marked this entrance for the sun-god.

Returning from the great wooden and stone sun-gateways of Durrington and Stonehenge, we come again to the gateway held open by the Long Man. More satisfying than the theory that he is a prehistoric surveyor or that he marks Roman units of land measurement, we see him instead as he truly is - a giant, a god, who comes from the south, the place of the maximum heat and light of the sun, and who faces the north, the place of the goddess and darkness. He stands holding open the gates of Time - the gates to the Underworld - but he stands also barring our way to that place within the hills.

Fig 6. Durrington rotunda

Again the words of Merlin's Prophecies come to mind. At the end of his visions, Merlin sees a time of chaos and dissolution, even amongst the stars: 'The Chariot of the Moon shall disturb the Zodiac, and the Pleiades shall burst into tears and lamentation. None hereafter shall return to his wonted duty, but Ariadne shall lie hidden within the closed gateways of her sea-girt headland.'

Robert Graves, in *The White Goddess*, believed that this referred to the sweeping away of the ancient Druid religion by Christianity. Whether this is so or not, and whether Merlin was speaking of events long past or still to come, the prophecy speaks of the disappearance of the goddess - of her hiding behind the closed gateways of the hills. And here, at just such a gateway stands the Long Man, on the Downs that indeed form part of that sea-girt headland that becomes the white cliffs of Beachy Head a few miles south-east before flattening into the Pevensey Levels between Eastbourne and Hastings.

And does the Long Man, known in the old days by some as the Lone Man, mourn her disappearance, wandering at night over to Hindover Hill, calling her name in the dark? Or was it he who, like most men, hid her in the depths of his own world - capturing her from her own land and imprisoning her here in Windover Hill? Does he stand at the gateway preventing us from penetrating the mysteries, from violating the goddess? Or does he stand guard to prevent her from escaping - to prevent her revealing the truth about the world?

In a sweeping statement of over-simplification and conjecture we could say that early Druidry - megalithic proto-Druidry - was probably matriarchal, moving towards a balance of both masculine and feminine forces, before becoming patriarchal as official Druidry suffered the inevitable corruption that ensues when the affairs of state become enmeshed with the affairs of religion. Druidry, like most religions, has experienced periods of growth and decay, of purity and corruption, of the rise of the feminine or the masculine power. Today, both within Druidry and within the wider context of society in general, we are witnessing a return of the feminine, a revival of an awareness of the goddess, that is redressing the balance in the collective psyche.

Humanity divorced from the feminine is shattered and divided. Slowly the World-Soul, like Isis seeking the fragments of Osiris' body, walks the earth collecting the pieces of our dismembered humanity until we can be whole again.

Osiris was killed by Seth and cut into pieces, which were then scattered throughout Egypt. Isis found all the parts of his body, except his phallus which had fallen into the Nile and had been eaten by fish, or in some versions, a crab.

And here, on a hillside in England, stands a god who also has no phallus. His lack of such an important appendage at one level may have a simple explanation. Our clue to when it may well have disappeared comes from the account of Dr.J.S.Phené who 'discovered' the Long Man in the 1870's and who initiated the marking out of the giant's outline in yellowish-white bricks at the expense of the Duke of Devonshire, and under the direction of the Revd. de St.Croix. When he visited the Cerne giant he found that he could only do so by 'overcoming with difficulty his repugnance at inspecting that figure.' The Cerne Giant was and still is marked out by trenches cut into the turf, and every bit of him was there on the hillside for all to see - and find repugnant if they so chose.

The Lone, Long, Lanky Man (all local names for him) was until the time of the marking-out in bricks, actually a Green Man. If he was originally a classic chalk hill figure cut into the turf, then the periodical scouring needed to stop the grass encroaching on his outline must have been abandoned many centuries previously and as a result he was a god who appeared on the hillside only under certain conditions. Up until the nineteenth century he was often known as the Green Man of Wilmington.

Covered in grass, the Green God would appear only at early morning or late evening on certain days when there was sufficient sun at the right angle. After it had snowed, he would appear briefly as the snow thawed, since the snow stayed a little longer in the shallow recesses of his outline than on the surrounding grass.

Mrs Ann Downs, who lived opposite the Long Man, at Wilmington Priory, from 1850 to 1860 felt that rebuilding his outline in brick was insensitive: 'Day after day, she used to look across to the secretive coombe where the Giant lay hidden under his blankets of soil and grass, watching as he appeared and disappeared in the changing light. She felt that the Giant was a secret being who was to be seen only at certain times.' (Rodney Castleden, *The Wilmington Giant*).

When the green giant became the white giant an error was made in the outline of one foot: both Mrs Downs' writings and photographs taken before the hurried bricking of 1874 indicate that the giant originally had both feet pointing down the slope - as if he was coming down the hillside or standing on tiptoe. But in the restoration, one foot was made to turn to the left - making the figure look as if it belongs to an Egyptian frieze. Since the restorers were able to make such a gross error with one foot, and since Dr Phené found the Cerne giant's phallus so repugnant, it seems highly likely that any markings in the grass around the Long Man's groin would have been overlooked. Indeed, to this day there is a clear indentation on this part of the giant, although this could have been caused by generations of men and women sitting there in the hope of becoming more fertile.

Archaeological work is due to be carried out at the end of 2004 which may help to date the figure, and trenches are due to be excavated around the head, groin and leg areas which will hopefully provide us with more clues as to its original appearance, and perhaps gender.

Both St Croix and Phené believed that the Long Man was actually used as an enclosure for mass Druidic executions or sacrifice. Lunatic though this suggestion may seem, we can understand their logic: Caesar and Strabo both mentioned that the Gauls constructed giants made of osiers, which they filled with men and set on fire. Since a wicker giant is a highly improbable structure, which would have collapsed rapidly as soon as the fire burnt the lower portions of it, St Croix and Phené suggested that perhaps the Long Man was just such a wicker giant: his outline being formed by a wicker fence which acted as a compound for the victims. Caesar landed only six miles away at Pevensey, and therefore may have witnessed such an event. But on examination, we realise that this idea is absurd. On the northern slope of Windover Hill, at an angle of 28 degrees, the Long Man is at a difficult gradient to negotiate at the best of times, and as Rodney Castleden points out: 'A complicated, repeatable rite involving the manhandling of prisoners, the building of a wooden palisade solid enough to thwart the victim's attempts to escape and the carrying of firewood to make bonfires inside the enclosure would be absurdly difficult on a slope of that steepness. There would, in addition, be every chance that both fences and bonfires would, once set on fire, collapse down the hillside, releasing the victims. The archaeological work on the site, slight though it has been, would have revealed signs of scorching and traces of charcoal over the outline. Needless to say, it has not.'

If St Croix and Phené were responsible for the disappearance, or more accurately the failure to restore, the giant's penis then they were not the only players in the strange game of 'Hide and Seek John Thomas' that has gone on in this area for some time.

In the 1890's a wealthy American from New England, Edward Warren, bought Lewes House, and developed a 'brotherhood of aesthetes' who began to collect antiquities that were to form the basis of the great classical collections at the Boston Museum of Fine Arts and the Metropolitan Museum in New York. At one point, six of the Lewes Brotherhood were living in the house, sharing hats and coats in common, swimming naked in the community pool and riding on Arab horses followed by a pack of St.Bernards. One of the members astonished locals by wearing a turkish fez in the High Street and addressing them in Arabic. But despite their eccentricities, the brotherhood were in touch with, or entertained at Lewes House, many of the leading writers and artists of the day, including Henri Matisse, Gertrude Stein, Oscar Wilde, Augustus John, Evelyn Waugh, H.G.Wells, Rebecca West and the Sitwells.

The sculptor Auguste Rodin was also a guest at the house, and from him Edward Warren commissioned a version of his famous sculpture, The Kiss. He insisted that Rodin take no longer than eighteen months to complete the statue, and that the man's genitals were to be seen 'in their entirety'. In the end, Rodin took four years to finish it, and though the man's penis is visible, it is hardly distinct. The sculpture was housed in the coach house of Lewes House until in 1914 Warren arranged to have it exhibited in the Town Hall. He planned to eventually donate it to the town of Lewes. It was placed in a corner of the assembly room used for concerts, but it was soon shrouded in black cloth. Young soldiers were present at the concerts in the assembly rooms, and the town fathers felt that exposure to such a statue would have 'a prurient effect' on them. Its weight - four tons - prevented its early removal, and it took three years before it was finally shifted back to the coach house, to be sold in 1953 to the Tate Gallery in London.

The town's prudish rejection of Warren's generous offer was finally expiated by a special Rodin exhibition in Lewes town hall in 1999, with The Kiss returning triumphant for five months, together with a specially commissioned play about the town's relationship to this extraordinary sculpture.

The sculptor Eric Gill lived in nearby Ditchling, and in 1932 a curious row developed over the figure of Ariel that Gill had carved above the entrance to Broadcasting House in Langham Place. At a preview of the carving behind a tarpaulin, the shocked governors of the BBC asked Gill to immediately reduce the size of Ariel's penis. Another carving of his was banned from a shop in Bond Street because a penis was present, and Gill's friend, Jacob Epstein, discovered the problems artists encounter in portraying the male nude, when there was a public outcry after the unveiling of his frieze depicting naked men and women for the British Medical Association building in the Strand. Undeterred,

Epstein and Gill spent one summer planning a twentieth-century Stonehenge in the Sussex landscape. They wanted to sculpt a series of immense naked human figures, which would stand like gods and giants in the rolling Downland. They even researched a site, a six-acre plot with a farmhouse, Asheham House, four miles from Lewes, but their plan never materialized. The following year, Vanessa Bell and her sister Virginia (soon to become Virginia Woolf) rented Asheham House for the winter. An enterprising Lewes Council, keen to develop the area's associations with sculpture, may yet revive this extraordinary plan with a new generation of sculptors.

One can find many stories of the hiding, diminution or removal of male genitalia in the history of art, and so superficially we can say that the Long Man has no 'Tree of Life' (another of the dozens of colloquial English synonyms for the penis) because of mere prudishness, but there are deeper mysteries here. The Trickster of certain Native American tribes is able to remove his phallus and carry it around in a box, but in England this ability was transferred from the man to the woman. Witches were said to be capable of removing men's penises, which they sometimes collected in great numbers, twenty or thirty at a time, hiding them in birds' nests or keeping them in boxes. In the boxes they would still be alive, moving about and feeding on oats and corn. They would then be handed out to male members of the coven for use in ceremonies.

Here we see a graphic depiction of the refusal to fully own, accept and take responsibility for creative and generative power: the genitalia have become alienated from the person, obviously in the case of the male, and in a disguised way in the case of the female, since boxes and birds' nests are known symbolisations of the vulva.

Reginald Scot, writing in *The Discovery of Witchcraft* in the sixteenth century, recounts one tale in which a young man, having been emasculated by a sorcerer, visits a witch for a cure. She tells him to climb a certain tree and to help himself from the organs he will find in the nest. He does this, and chooses the biggest and heaviest specimen, whereupon the witch tells him that he can choose any but that one - which is reserved for the parish priest. 'This,' says Scot, 'is no jest, for it is given credence by judges who passed sentence of death upon those who knew of this great treasure chest.'

Our amusement at this jibe at the parish priest turns to despair when we realise that women were burned and killed by men for supposedly engaging in such an activity: an accusation so preposterous that we cannot believe it could ever have been taken seriously. It is a classic example of 'misplaced concreteness': the emotional knowledge of men that they can be psychologically castrated and emasculated by women was transferred from its proper realm to fantasies of the concrete physical level, with the absurd and vicious consequences of women being killed.

So who has taken the Long Man's 'root of evil', 'ransacker', 'searcher', 'housebreaker', 'pusher', 'tearer'? Has he, like the Trickster, popped it in a box and hidden it, or has a wicked witch lopped it off and hidden it in her own box, where she feeds it still with seed from the fields around him?

The theme of the dismembered penis is universal. Several years back, I travelled to the run-down town of Ica, in the desert south of Lima, to see the famous Nazca Lines of Peru. There, in the main square I found a very odd museum. Run by Dr Cabrera and his assistant, the museum is filled to overflowing with black stones carved with extraordinary images that Dr Cabrera says were retrieved from a cave in the desert. On these stones we see heart transplants being performed, heads being trepanned (an operation in which a hole is made in the skull and which some modern day fanatics have repeated), and most extraordinary of all - images of men having their penises removed. Dr Cabrera believed that this operation was for 'spiritual' purposes - serving a similar end to trepanning. If people were prepared to drill holes in their head to get 'high' I suppose some of them might have considered removing their genitals for similar reasons. Certainly the early Christian father Origen did, when in another extraordinary act of misplaced concreteness, he took literally Jesus's words 'and there be eunuchs, which have made themselves eunuchs for the kingdom of heaven's sake' (Matthew 19:12). The Skoptsi, an obscure Christian sect in Russia which continued to exist up until the beginning of the 20th century, also took Jesus's words literally. I wonder how they would have taken it, if they were then told that a witch, rather than Jesus, had influenced them, and that they could retrieve their genitals from a nearby bird's nest?

So the removal of cocks by archaeologists, town councillors, workmen, ancient Peruvians, witches or Christians can at one level be put down to misplaced concreteness - a failure to appreciate the distinction between the inner and the outer, between internal dynamics and one particular physical organ.

But at another level, the appearance and disappearance of the phallus represents the cyclical nature of fertility: in the spring the phallus is adored erect in the Maypole, for with it comes the promise of the harvest. In the autumn, the harvest is cut down, and with it the man - symbolised this time by John Barleycorn. The god is cut down, the man is sacrificed, the penis withers from being proud like a tall tree, to being shrivelled like an autumn leaf. The earth lies dormant until the cycle repeats itself. Seen in this way, the Cerne Abbas Giant is the giant of spring and summer, while the Long Man is the giant of autumn and winter. Seen in this way too, we come to appreciate the cyclical or changeable nature of male sexuality or of man's psyche. Because of the limiting association of man with the sun and woman with the moon, we have tended to view masculinity as a constant, like the sun's light, with femininity as variable - like the moon. But this association has saddled men with the feeling that they are less than men if they are not always macho, continuously virile, just as it has saddled women with the belief that they are by nature fickle or changeable.

We think that women have periods, and that men don't, but this isn't true. Research at Stanford University on the testosterone cycle shows that men have a regular hormone cycle that relates consistently to their changing moods and emotions. The reality is that a man's sexuality is in many ways more fleeting, more fragile, than a woman's: before orgasm he is a rampant stag, afterwards a dormouse. In every act of intercourse the woman and man repeat the story of the earth: the tide of spring and of the rising sun flows through his cock, only to give way to the waning light of sunset and the coming autumn and winter. Men who feel this sensation within themselves sometimes experience it as 'post-coital tristesse' - a feeling of sadness immortalised by the classical author who wrote 'post-coitum omnia animalia trista sunt' (after coitus all animals are sad).

But as well as the two giants of Britain showing us the two faces of man that parallel the seasonal and agricultural cycles, we have in the image of the Long Man a symbol of androgyny. He is called a man, yet objectively the figure could equally be that of a woman. I interviewed members of the public who were picnicking by the figure for a TV feature about the first edition of this book, asking them whether they were looking at a man or a woman. Once the question was raised, no-one insisted it was a man. Women pointed to the figure's child-bearing hips which suggest she is a woman, and everyone agreed that the figure was ambiguous.

Has the Hindover goddess actually disappeared from the nearby hillside because both god and goddess have finally united in the *heiros gamos* and are now One? Like the final card in the Major Arcana of the Tarot, the World, which depicts a hermaphrodite, is the Long Man perhaps a vast message carved in the earth reminding us of the necessity to unite the opposites? He certainly seems to show this great goal in spiritual development in the way that he holds to either side of him those two staves like the great pillars of the Tree of Life, but perhaps he also shows us this in his lack of phallus. More than we can hope for in our times, he shows us the way beyond the particularity and drivenness of gender.

There is yet another image we must consider, though. The phallus, rather than being denied or detached, or transmuted in androgyny, is perhaps there - but wounded. For our present times this is the most powerful image in relation to man-as-we-find-him, and it is no coincidence that this image is found at the centre of the story of the Holy Grail. In the midst of the Wasteland lies the Fisher King in the Grail castle grievously wounded, and unable to heal himself or the land by drinking from the grail cup. Some texts say that he is wounded in the thigh, but in others this euphemism is made explicit: he is wounded in the genitals, his testes being transfixed by an arrow that cannot be removed. Here we see the man, the god, who has lost his mate and effectively his cock. He cannot unite with the feminine, the grail, and he has no generative power. As his seed dies, so does the land.

This belief in a connection between the fertility of the king and the fertility of the land is no mere superstition of a primitive people. In seeing the relationship between human seed and the seed of the earth, our ancestors were aware of our interdependence and of the foolishness of considering the two as separate. If we were to preserve the seed of the crops we were also to preserve our own seed. Perhaps we find here the relationship between our meddling with crop seed in genetic modification and the falling sperm count amongst western males.

One of the reasons for a warrior having to learn the

genealogies of the tribes, as did the Bards, was so that he could *know* his foe. His code of honour prevented him from striking a man until he knew that man's seed - only then did he have the right to end that seed - to interfere in its carriage across time. It is said that if he believed, from his knowledge of the genealogies, that man to carry bad seed, then he might kill him. But if his seed was good, he could only scar or wound him. What consciousness is implied in such a tradition of warriorhood! And what a comparison we can make to our modern 'civilisation' which kills instead with a complete lack of knowledge of the foe: by remote-control.

But to return to the image of the Fisher King, a little thought makes us realise that wounding is a theme that is not confined to the grail story. Jean Houston, in *The Search for the Beloved* lists over a dozen mythological woundings when she says:

> 'An abundance of sacred wounding marks the core of all great Western myths and their attending gods and humans: Adam's rib, Achilles' heel, Odin's eye, Orpheus's decapitation, Inanna's torture, Prometheus's liver, Zeus's split head, Pentheus's dismemberment, Job's boils, Jacob's broken hip, Isaiah's seared lips, Persephone's rape, Eros's burnt shoulder, Oedipus's blinding, Jesus' crucifixion. All of these myths of wounding carry with them the uncanny, the mysterious, *the announcement that the sacred is entering into time.* Each prefigures a journey, a renaissance, a birth or rebirth, a turning point in the lives of gods and mortals. In sacred psychology, the possibility for therapeia, for healing and wholing, seems to require acknowledgement and understanding of our deepest wounds.'

Jean Houston clarifies this necessity for an acknowledgement of our wounding by suggesting that it is only through wounding that our boundaries are enlarged, that our psyche is opened up and 'new questions begin to be asked about who we are in our depths':

> 'As seed making begins with the wounding of the ovum by sperm, so does soulmaking begin with the wounding of the psyche by the Larger Story. *Soulmaking requires that you die to one story to be reborn to a larger one*. A renaissance, a rebirth, occurs not just because there is a rising of ancient and archetypal symbols. A renaissance happens because the soul is breached.'

What it is essential for us to understand now at this particular time in human history is that the wounding has occurred not only to ourselves, but to the world. Not only is Self wounded, but Other is too. This is the radical shift we have to make in awareness. Like Janus we must look both ways now: inside and outside, for both our inner and outer worlds are hurt and in the acknowledgement of the woundedness of one, we can perhaps find an ability to acknowledge the wounding in the other.

How similar is the denial by politicians of the urgency of the environmental crisis to the denial of an individual who is clearly in psychological crisis but refuses to admit it. In Paul Simon's song, Fat Charlie, the Archangel had to discover that his life was on fire by reading about it in the evening news. Fat Charlie the politician will discover that he can't breathe when he's briefed about this by his aides. Shepherds in Patagonia are given sunglasses to stop them going blind - they would give the sheep sunglasses too, but there are too many of them and they are going blind already. One in four Australians develop skin cancer. There is a serious thinning of the ozone layer over Europe. We fail to acknowledge the woundedness of the planet as we fail to acknowledge our own woundedness. 'Don't tell him he's dying!' we exhort the visitor to the deathbed in a hospital - encouraging the ultimate cowardice and stupidity of denial.

Realising that an acknowledgement of woundedness is a prerequisite to being healed and becoming whole, we can now look at the particular version of woundedness that is presented to us in the images and stories of men, gods and giants wounded in their genitalia, for it is not only the Fisher King who is damaged in this way: Cronus cut off the penis of his father Uranus and threw it into the sea, Attis, born of the almond tree, emasculated himself in a frenzy, Adonis is mortally wounded in the groin, as is Cheiron, and Jacob in the 'thigh' - often taken as code for the genitals.

Where on earth do all these stories spring from? There are clearly a number of levels of interpretation, all of which are valid within their own parameters, but which become misleading when applied inappropriately.

Freudian psychology would see in these myths evidence of the castration anxiety which it believes plays a formative role in male psychosexual development. The theory goes that the little boy notices that his mother and girls have no penis. He may also notice that his mother bleeds in menstruation. Clearly she, and all other females, have had their penises cut off. It might happen to him if he is naughty! The best strategy is to ally himself with his father, who has still got his and is therefore stronger, rather than his mother, who is wounded. Prior to this, the boy had a passionate but aimless sensual attachment to his mother, but it was his father who cuddled up in bed with her. So he hated him and wanted to kill him so his mother could be his, and his alone - the Oedipus complex! But then along came the castration complex which Freud saw as helping the boy identify with his own sex, seeking an alliance with the father, rather than the mother. In this way the castration complex provides, to some degree, a resolution of the Oedipus complex.

To many, these ideas seem farcical - and particularly the related theory of penis envy which Freud saw in women, since he believed them, as little girls, to come to the same conclusion as little boys - that they were castrated. Psychological research over the last forty years has shown, however, that there is good evidence for the existence of both the Oedipus and castration complexes, whereas there is no firm evidence for penis envy. Although research has determined the existence of Oedipal and castration complexes in men, it is important to note that this does not mean that Freud's explanation of the origin of these complexes is necessarily valid.

Whether or not Freudian theory is correct, at least as regards male psychology, it can only explain one layer of meaning in relation to this powerful image. At a deeper, universal, level these myths present us with allegories of seasonal renewal - in winter-time the goddess is hidden in the Underworld, the god is emasculated; the forces of fertility are apparently dead, only to reappear again in the spring. In this understanding, the gods are seen as personifications of natural forces: emasculated gods such as Attis and Adonis being seen as vegetation gods. Whether their cocks are cut down or whether as Corn Gods their whole bodies are cut down, they symbolise the necessity for death in order for rebirth to occur. Some historians say that the crucifix was originally a phallic symbol, and this suggests that the death of Jesus portrays a similar story of the dying of the generative powers in order that they might return (fittingly at springtime – Easter).

Another level of meaning opens to us when we consider the image of the castrated or penis-less male as symbolic of sublimation rather seasonal death. John Layard in *A Celtic Quest* has analysed in detail the themes of that primordial grail and Arthurian tale from the *Mabinogion*, the story of Culhwch and Olwen. Replete with images of castration, the story is about how Culhwch wins Olwen as a bride by accomplishing, with the help of King Arthur, seemingly impossible tasks set for him by Olwen's father, the giant Ysbaddaden Penkawr. At the end of the story the giant is shaved, from ear to ear, and he gives his daughter to Culhwch. After this symbolic castration, the giant says 'And it is high time to take away my life' at which point he is decapitated and 'that night Culhwch slept with Olwen, and she was his only wife so long as he lived. And the hosts of Arthur dispersed, every one to his country.' Layard suggests that castration symbolically can have both positive and negative meanings. Negatively it is seen as unwilling sacrifice, but positively it means the 'voluntary sacrifice of unrestrained natural libido for the sake of acquiring inner control and ultimate spiritual union (the *heiros gamos*) with the anima.' Here we see the act of denying masculinity, in the sense of outwardly directed male sexuality, as a means of directing the fertilising power inward and upward. The dangers of either acting with misplaced concreteness (i.e. actually lopping it off) or of the imbalance and delusion that unexpressed male sexuality can engender, are all too well documented.

Instead of being a symbol for the man seeking 'inner control and ultimate spiritual union' (or 'curbing [his] primary externally expressed natural desire in order to produce an inner experience' as Layard also puts it) the emasculated man can become a symbol of the disempowered man - the man separated from his natural function, from his nature as a fertilising being. Like a gelding he is rendered docile and amenable. He has been tamed. If the Long Man is the Gelding, the Cerne Abbas Giant is his opposite - the Wild Man.

Further levels of interpretation open to us when we consider the image of the sexless man as in fact hermaphroditic or androgynous, as we have discussed previously. William Blake said 'The Ancients wrote it in the earth', and what more eloquent statement of our yearning for completeness is there than the image of the Long Man-Woman of Wilmington?

The image of a hermaphrodite can either have no breasts and no penis, or both. If the restorers of 1874 overlooked the traces of a phallus, perhaps they overlooked also the traces of breasts?

We can imagine that if Phené found a cock repugnant, how much more revolting he would have found a cock and breasts on the same figure! But whether this was the case or not, the present status of the Long Man as the Sexless One acts as an important statement for our times. In 1968 there were 3.5 billion people on the planet, only thirty or so years on there are 6 billion. Our problem is no longer one of needing to be fertile: as beings we are excessively good at production.

We produce too many cars, too many bombs, too many things and too many people for our own and everything else's good. However, the statistics on the increasing levels of infertility in Western populations, combined with observing the effects on human, animal and plant fertility from increased solar radiation due to depletion of the ozone layer, all show that just as our seed has enabled our population to expand to unmanageable proportions, so - at least in part of the world - it is now refusing to, or becoming incapable of cooperating in this suicidal agenda. One writer, Michael Poynder, even believes that we shall soon all become infertile. The paradox we are faced with is that in order to preserve life, we must now seek not to engender it - each of us then enacts the myth of the vegetation, corn or sacrificial god in our own small way. And when we die, each of us in the end, male or female, becomes the corn god: 'Man that is born of a woman hath but a short time to live.... he cometh up and is cut down like a flower'.

Seen in this way, the Long Man becomes a symbol of the contemporary need for us to find a new sexuality that is not directed towards fertility in a reproductive sense - hence the reproductive organs are not shown: the generative power being transferred to the hands which hold the staves. The hands have always symbolised sublimated or transmuted sexual energy for it is the hands which fertilise the world of culture, rather than the human race, through their acts of writing, painting, sculpting and directing.

Our tendency is to view symbols and myths as frozen in time, and attempt to understand them from a distance. But Lévi-Strauss in his classic essay 'The Structural Study of Myth' suggested instead that we should bring all variants of a myth together in a single imaginary space without a concern for their historical context: 'We define the myth as consisting of all its versions... Therefore, not only Sophocles, but Freud himself, should be included among the recorded versions of the Oedipus myth on a par with earlier or seemingly more "authentic" versions.' In other words, the Arthurian mythos includes not only the works of Malory but also of Marion Bradley, and also the Arthurian poem you yourself may have written. The Long Man may have originally been created with a phallus or without one, but today he is without one and as such speaks to us in a particular way, and however each of us receives or interprets this message becomes part of his story, part of the myth that this particular landscape weaves for us all.

We have seen how the image of the corn or vegetation god can be portrayed either as dead or simply as cock-less - both images showing that he can no longer transmit life. The Long Man of Wilmington can therefore be seen today in this way too - as a harvest god, a corn god. But for me, the sadness that I experience at Wilmington is that this symbol of the male who cannot procreate is filled with millennial, apocalyptic overtones. For the first time in the history of humanity there is the possibility that the corn god may be cut down for the last time. All of us alive at this present time are truly at a Gateway, and we cannot be sure any longer of where the river of life will flow. In the churchyard nearby there is a profound sense of the stream of life that flows from the very earliest of days up to the present. And here the present, not the future, is all-powerful, for the god is telling us that we have come to a particular moment in history - a moment of harvest, when we are about to reap the consequences of years of desecration of the land, years of desecration of our bodies and souls.

And the Gateway of Yews in the churchyard is truly a gateway I hope we never cross.

Shaman
(for John Agard)

Is this the way dawn
comes in your country -
a hushed leaning,
a breathing-out of
forgotten gods?

With your snake eyes
your hands flicking
like knotted lightning
you conjure
the single shy flower
out of our deserts

with your raven voice
your panther silence
you sing back
the green ghosts from childhood
that we have banished.

Poetry is a word for it.
we have not looked but
there is something new
in this room
walking with us -

soul, nakedness, our
severed knowledge.
Tonight, in Brixton
they are burning, maiming
looting for lack of it.

In Iran now
petrol bombs bloom orange
over ruins that were once
its oracle;
all our history has come down
to this:

Heart, without you
our world is narrower
and more lethal than
a knifepoint;
there must be no more shrinking.

going home beneath
icy stars, I pray:
snake, raven, panther
river of steep shadow
do not desert us

Stephen Parr

The Goddess

I wait for my love in the
twilit shadow
the halfway shadow:
sweet of the meadow,
hedgerose under cattle feet.
Scooped plank is soft in
the dusk..

Over the days that passed after my return to Lewes, I was haunted not only by the image of the Long Man, but even more so by the image of the goddess who had spoken to me. Again and again I saw her tear-streaked face and heard Nuinn's voice shouting at me "Look at her! She is the Goddess who has been denied. She is the soul of every one of us who watches the world destroyed before our very eyes."

One evening as I fell asleep, I was given a way of travelling into the Other World by the Long Man himself which would allow me to meet her again. I began my voyage into sleep by thinking of that strange lonely giant on the hillside - seeing him in my mind's eye and ruminating on how in many ways he is an insubstantial figure, a perfect image to evoke unconscious material because of his very lack of substance. One of the tricks of psychoanalysis is for the analyst to make him or herself insubstantial, a 'blank screen', a Long Person, which consequently evokes projection of material from the unconscious of the patient. Since it seems that we cannot bear blankness, emptiness, we supply the content - if the analyst won't.

But whereas conventional psychology treats every experience in consciousness as personal and particular to the individual experiencing it, esoteric, sacred or transpersonal psychology recognises the existence of 'other realms' or 'inner realms' which are independent of the individual experiencing them. And what happened as I drifted between waking and sleeping was that the Long Man told me that he could be a blank screen for my own unconscious material, or he could be a gatekeeper and a way-shower to inner realms which are independent and separate from my own personal inner realm. I asked if I could be shown this second, more interesting way of working, and he told me: "All you have to do is look at both of my staves." I tried this, and to begin with found it impossible - I could only focus on one stave at a time. But soon I discovered there was a way: I had to focus my inner eye directly in between the two staves - only then could I see both staves together. And to do all this I had to relax my gaze - I couldn't do it with a stare, I had to make my vision receptive: I had to let go in some way. As I did this, I found myself gazing into an inner world that glowed darkly ahead of me. And in this velvet darkness I saw the figure of the goddess, seated on a throne.

It is easiest for us to enter other realms in that delicious state between waking and sleeping, and whether I 'left my body', entered the Otherworld or fell asleep and began dreaming I do not know, but whatever happened I found myself standing before the goddess. Although she wore the same torn dark clothes in which I had seen her a few days previously at Wilmington, she looked older, larger.

I found myself trembling again in her presence. "Who are you?" I asked.

"I am the goddess denied," she began to say, "I have been

called by many names by countless men and women. I am Brighid and Ana, Isis and Astarte, Venus and Diana. All you need to know is that until you come to me, until you accept me in your heart, you will never truly be a man." And then I cannot fully describe what happened, my sense of being a separate entity in the universe dissolved - I seemed to become all of it, or it all of me. The distinction between me and not me, between subject and object, disappeared for a while as an awareness of the whole world, all of humanity, flooded into my consciousness before I drifted into a deep sleep.

When I woke up the next morning, I found that during the night I had scribbled on my bedside pad "Go back to Wilmington - there is something you haven't discovered yet."

In a few weeks' time it would be Alban Eilir, Light of the Earth, the time of the spring equinox. I decided to go then.

The day was glorious. The sun was shining brilliantly, and there were only tiny white clouds here and there in the clear blue sky. As I set off from the Priory, the Long Man and the surrounding landscape were bathed in light and shining brightly - white and green. There was no sadness here. I started to doubt my feelings of sadness and millennial gloom - maybe they had just originated from my own fatigue and my own psyche. Soon I was beside the dewpond again. Over to the left I noticed a cluster of beech trees which looked from the distance like a small grove. Walking there I discovered them to form not quite a grove, but even so any group of trees creates its own force-field or aura - and here was a strong sense of a unified field of energy, a collective Tree Spirit perhaps.

And within this magical tree-cluster was a small circle of flint-stones - beautifully arranged by a previous visitor. Each stone with its bulbous base and lumpy protrusions looked like an ancient statue of the Mother Goddess dredged up from the sea-bed. I said a prayer to the Mother Goddess, sat on a log and gazed back at the Long Man. But he was no longer there.

That old Druid Winston Churchill has said that most of us stumble over the truth, pick ourselves up and walk on. The secret is to stop and stare. But even then we can be deceived because reality is multi-layered. We have to keep looking - again and again. Last time I had looked at the Long Man the obvious tumbled into my awareness - that he was not fully a man. But now as I looked I saw deeper into the obvious - the obvious that is 'written in the earth' for all of us to see - THE LONG MAN IS NOT A MAN - HE'S A WOMAN! HE IS NOT A MIGHTY GOD CARVED ON THE HILLSIDE - SHE IS A GODDESS. Go there and look and you will see: at the groin there is that depression in the earth like a vulva, and the hips are clearly female not male. Perhaps the angle of viewing and the early morning sun that equinoctial day helped to emphasise these features - but they are undoubtedly there whatever the sun is doing.

Whether or not the figure was originally drawn to represent a man or woman is not so important as the fact that now - today - for whatever reason - the figure here at Wilmington is of a woman not a man.

We make a mistake if we see our heritage, whether it be the Druid Tradition or our ancient monuments, as frozen in time. Levi-Strauss's understanding of myth can be applied to every aspect of our inheritance - each is alive and growing and changing. Today, here in Sussex, we have a mighty goddess carved on the Downs. She is The Long Woman of Wilmington. Just as the psychoanalyst becomes the person we need by treading lightly in relationship, so this great figure has become the image we need by treading lightly too on the earth.

How fitting it is that as patriarchy dies around us, the Goddess should re-emerge out of the very earth and grass.

Filled with exuberance, I no longer felt this place to be one of denial and discontinuity, of emasculation and castration and of the dying corn-god, but instead here was a place of bounty and beauty, where the gentle curving femininity of the downland landscape was matched by the femininity of the figure carved upon it.

When planning the next stage of the journey the previous week, I had decided to walk to Hindover Hill, now called High and Over, to search for the Lone Man's mate - to see if I could pick up traces of the goddess that had once apparently been honoured there. But right at the beginning, here on this spring morning, the morning of the Light of the Earth, I had in some ways already found her shining in and on and out of the earth. Nevertheless I decided to continue in search of her older companion.

Climbing up the hillside over to the left of the Long Woman, I was soon as high as the hawk again - gazing out at sweeping views across Avronelle and Anderida far below. Turning off the South Downs Way for a little while, and following another track, I soon came to a tumulus. Standing on this, I could just see Lewes, tucked behind Mount Caburn far to the west, while down below to my right I could see the Pevensey Levels - a great area of flat land stretching almost to Hastings, which lay on the eastern horizon. Here the South Downs end and I realised that the Long Woman of Wilmington stands guard at the beginning of this range of hills. She stands, one hand on each pillar, at the gateway of this ancient track that leads to the other gateways at one of the hearts of Logres - on Salisbury Plain. Perhaps one of the reasons for carving such a figure was to act as a marker for the gathering of pilgrims bound for Stonehenge.

Returning to the South Downs Way, walking over the broad back of the hill I soon found myself coming to Friston forest and the Lullington Heath Nature Reserve which lies above it. Both these places are good examples of modern conservation work. It is easy to fall into the trap of viewing modern man as rapacious in relation to the environment and ancient man as being 'in tune' with the environment. But this idealistic view of our ancestors is not borne out by the evidence: the Hopi Indians totally destroyed all their forests, and Early Iron Age man had probably cleared England of 50 per cent of its woodland by 500 BCE. Our onslaught against the trees is as old as humanity.

But here at Friston, the Forestry Commission has planted a big forest - partly with the aim of protecting underground water supplies from pollution. And to the north of the forest is the nature reserve, which preserves the heathland habitat for such birds as the linnet, dunnock, yellowhammer and stonechat, and butterflies such as the Adonis blue, chalkhill blue and the silver-spotted skipper. Walking through the reserve, there are violets amongst the brambles and grasses, and white cabbage butterflies dance over the furze that is already beginning to flower.

And then the forest looms ahead... all the land here feels special, as if by travelling behind the Goddess of Wilmington we are entering her territory, her inner landscape. Not wanting to enter a dark forest on such a sunny day, it was good to find it criss-crossed with wide grass swathes. But such criss-crossing means you are endlessly faced with cross-roads. Each time you must make a choice about which way to turn.

And as I choose each turn at each crossroad, it feels as if I am entering deeper and deeper into the goddess, deeper and deeper into my feminine self. This journeying towards the feminine is something that has preoccupied me for most of my life: for years it was the search for my outer feminine counterpart, the search for the beloved. Gradually that was replaced by an exploration of the feminine within, but now it seems as if I am exploring the feminine in the very landscape itself.

One way of understanding the importance for a man to search for his inner feminine self, is to realise that each man has a feminine component in his psyche which acts as an interior companion or inspirer. It is this companion which is depicted in myth as the fair damsel, and which in a man's creative life acts as his muse. In his sexual life it is this aspect of his psyche which shows him how to be gentle, subtle and open in his attitudes and feelings and in the way he makes love, to balance his maleness which is vigorous rather than gentle, overt rather than subtle, and focussed and penetrative rather than open. In Jungian psychology this feminine component is termed the *anima* and in myth and story we see her portrayed as Dante's Beatrice, Parsifal's Blanche Fleur, or Don Quixote's Dulcinea.

The authorship of *Don Quixote* is now being thrown into doubt: there is a theory that an Englishman rather than the Spaniard Miguel de Cervantes wrote the 900 page work which was first published in 1605. A number of features suggest an English, rather than Spanish setting for the tale.

Early in the story Don Quixote's library is burnt by the local priest and barber whilst his niece and cook look on, and while Don Quixote is fast asleep. This is reminiscent of the sacking of Dr John Dee's library in 1583 at Mortlake in Surrey. John Dee, who was Queen Elizabeth I's astrologer, also had a strong interest in our ancient heritage. When Dee was living in Wales at Nant-y-Groes he presented a petition to Lord Burleigh to be granted whatever treasure he might find when he excavated local tumuli, and Dr William Aubrey, grandfather of John Aubrey, the diarist in many ways responsible for the English Druid Revival in the 17th century, had been a friend and neighbour of Dee when he had lived in Kew. While Dee was travelling abroad and following the advice of spirits to engage in wife-swapping with his alchemist friend Kelley, the local populace decided that his library was too dangerous, thereby destroying a good deal, though not all, of the most complete collection in its day of scientific, magical and esoteric books in Britain.

When Don Quixote's library was destroyed, his niece told him that an 'enchanter' had arrived during the night, riding on a dragon. Don Quixote knew who he was: Freston – 'a very wise Inchanter':

> *"It was not the Divell, said his Niese, but an Inchanter that came here one night upon a cloude, the day after you departed from hence; and alighting downe from a Serpent upon whiche he rode, he entred into the Studie, and what he did therein I know not; and within a while after, he fledde out at the roofe of the house, and left all the house full of smoake: and when we accorded to see what he had done, we could neyther see booke or Studie: onely this much the old woman. And I doe remember very well, that the naughty olde man at his departure, said with a loud voyce, that he, for hidden enmitie, that he bore to the Lord of those bookes, had done all the harme to the house: that they might perceive when he were departed, and added that he was named the wise Muniaton. Freston, you would have said, quoth Don-Quixote. I know not, quoth the old woman, whether he hight Freston or Friton, but well I wot, that his name ended with Ton. That is true, quoth Don-Quixote, and he is a very wise Inchanter."*

By stressing the 'ton' word ending, the author is drawing our attention to the names Muniaton and Freston, and is also pointing out the Englishness of these names: no surnames or place-names in Spanish have such an ending, whereas they are common in England, since the ending derives from the Anglo-Saxon word for farm.

Freston was the old name for Friston, and the odd word Muniaton may be a combination of the spanish *muniaco* - a male figure - and Aton or Aten the Egyptian Sun-god. The

Long Man is peculiarly reminiscent of an Egyptian bas-relief figure, and Rodney Castleden has suggested that since the existence of trade between Bronze Age southern England and the Eastern mediterranean is now seen as highly likely, the design of the Long Man may have indeed originated in Egypt. He can certainly be seen as a sun-god, since he comes from the South and to face him we must face the full strength of the midday sun. Muniaton - the Sun-god Man - seems a highly fitting name for the hillside god near Friston.

Soon after learning of Muniaton's or Freston's destruction of the library, we read of the famous encounter between Don Quixote and the windmills, which he takes to be giants. Sancho Panza tries to point out that these are not giants, just windmills, but poor old Sancho doesn't understand the world of his master:

> 'I pray you understand, quoth Sancho Panza, that those which appear there, are no Gyants but Windemils: and that which seemes in them to be armes, are their Sayles, that are swinged about by the Winde, doe also make the Mill goe. It seems well, quoth Don Quixote, that thou art not yet acquainted with matter of adventures: they are Gyants, and if thou beest afeard, goe aside and pray, whilst I enter into cruell and unequall battell with them.'

The inevitable happens and Don Quixote's lance is shattered by the whirling sails which lift him and his horse high in the air, hurling them both to the ground in a heap. Sancho rushes to his master, furious with him for having been so stupid, but Don Quixote is philosophical and knows who is behind this dastardly trick of turning the giants at the final moment into machines: 'Peace, Sancho, quoth Don-Quixote, for matters of warre are more subject then any other thing to continuall change: how much more seeing I do verily perswade my self, that the wise Freston who robbed my Studie and bookes, hath transformed these Giants into Mils...'

The Downs were once home to dozens of windmills - their elevated and exposed flanks offering ideal sites. Sussex alone had more than sixty of them by 1724. There was once a windmill on Windover Hill - just above the Long Man, as there was on Firle Beacon. Located just beside Hunter's Burgh long barrow, the Windover Windmill was burnt down in the 1880's, but its foundations can still be seen as a circular bank of raised earth. The giants of Firle and Windover by the time *Don Quixote* was written had indeed been changed from characters of local legend to giant machines waving their arms in the wind. The famous episode that is 'quintessentially Quixotic' and is so well known, succeeds in conveying in just one incident, just one image, the transition from the mythic to the scientific way of perceiving the world. If we relate it to the downland landscape, the image also accurately portrays the local metamorphosis of the familiar giants into the giant machines that usurped them.

And here by Friston Forest lies Friston Place, built in the fifteenth century and therefore in existence at the time *Don Quixote* was written. It is tempting to think of the author staying there, walking the downland and finding his inspiration in the windmills and tales of local giants and dragons.

Walking through the forest I came to Snap Hill, and thought I saw wise Friston the Enchanter mounting his dragon steed - there was a rush of smoke and air and they were both gone. Looking from the hill in the direction of Alfriston I could see only the purple haze of bare woodland against the Downs, framed by an avenue of beech and Scots pine. I then walked down this avenue to Charleston Bottom, swinging left to come to the wide green sward of the valley floor.

The forest itself seems almost exclusively created with beech and Scots pine, but here and there I saw juniper and hawthorn. Scots pine has a powerful presence, and its height and unusual silhouette seem to have selected it as a natural marker at certain points along the Straight Tracks. Alfred Watkins first noticed the way in which these trees, either individually or in a cluster, seem to be used as ley mark points, and it was not only in Britain that they were considered of special significance. Mirov and Hasbrouck in *The Story of Pines* recount how 'The Buriats, a Mongolian people living around the southern end of Lake Baikal in East Siberia, often viewed Scots pine groves as sacred. These 'shaman forests' were scattered over dry grassland. Before the Soviet revolution of 1917, one approached and rode through the groves in silence lest the gods and spirits of the woods be offended.'

Here in the Enchanter's Forest of Friston many of the pines have honeysuckle clinging to them. Honeysuckle, *Uilleand* in Irish, is one of the family of sacred trees of the Ogham Alphabet, that secret tree-language of the Druids popularised in poetic and esoteric circles by Robert Graves' *The White Goddess.* Calling the Ogham a tree alphabet is really a misnomer, since at least six of the group are not really trees at all: being furze and heather, ivy and vine, reed and honeysuckle. Some authors include broom, gorse, bramble, gooseberry, fern and elecampane (a plant of the same family as the sunflower). Hernan Turner in Eire solves the naming difficulty by calling the Ogham a woodland, rather than a tree, alphabet. And here in this woodland are a number of the non-tree members of this special group: bramble and furze, heather and ivy. A few miles away are vines galore at Breakey Bottom - home of some of the best English wine.

The honeysuckle winds its way up into the high boughs of the pine, reminding me, in its clinging, that prudish mothers banned it from their homes in the fenlands: for the way the stems of the barebind or woodbine, as it was known, entwine each other was too reminiscent of the lovers' embrace, and it was believed that it gave young girls erotic dreams. But understood in its inner sense, and when used in divination, the honeysuckle indicates the possibility of discovering a hidden secret, and that we must use our discrimination not to be distracted in our search. The bird associated with *Uilleand* is the lapwing, and when it is nesting it will fly up and away when disturbed, uttering a distinctive cry to draw any potential predator's attention away from its eggs. The eggs represent the secret, the treasure. In marvelling at the height and the tenderness with which the *Uilleand* hugs the pine, I take this as a sign to use discrimination and to be attentive to any hidden secrets that may lie ahead.

The path along Charleston Bottom leads finally to the road, and crossing this I join the Heritage Coastal Path which runs alongside the Cuckmere river. Here in the rivulet that you first encounter on the path, is another member of the Ogham family: *Ngetal*, the Reed. Liz and Colin Murray, in *The Celtic Tree Oracle* say 'In his thinness the reed resembles arrows that fly, silver-tipped, up into the unknown air to land at the very source that one had searched for all these years.'

Climbing over a stile, the willow-fringed path beside the rivulet leads to the Cuckmere itself: a lazy river whose water flows so slowly that it seems almost unnaturally glassy. It meanders through a wide and totally flat valley that is bordered on either side by the Downs.

I had few hopes of finding the Long Man's lost mate, the goddess of Hindover. Of all the writings on the Long Man and on this region that I had studied, I had found only one fleeting reference to her, in a book of folklore, tucked away in the library of the Sussex Archaeological Society. It would be unlikely that any clues would be left in the countryside itself.

But as I walked beside the Cuckmere, or Snake River as it has been called, I looked across the water to Hindover Hill, and there she was - not hidden, not hidden at all...

The Longing of Return

And I knew then why I long to nestle my head between your thighs.
It is the longing of Return.
And I knew then why you love to feed from the white milk of generation.
It is the longing of Manna.

May I be born again,
May you be fed forever.
May the Serpent Ouroborous forever show us
that feeding and giving are eternally the same.

Hindover Hill, now called High & Over, is known for the magnificent view its summit gives of the Cuckmere Valley, with its snakey river that winds its way towards the sea and the white cliffs of the Seven Sisters. And it is known too for its chalk horse carved in the earth in 1838 and then again in 1925, to commemorate a girl who was killed when her horse bolted downhill and threw her.

Facing the hill you see the horse, now somewhat overgrown but clearly visible near the summit. To the right the hill curves in on itself before another flank bends outwards again. And within this curve lies a natural triangle of woodland. To either side the bare downland slopes stretch out towards Snake River like great thighs of the Goddess.

Where the thighs converge there is the Place of Mystery, the Hidden Doorway, the luxuriant furry wooded realm that we emerged from when born and which many of us long to return to.

I crossed over Snake River, and walked up to this most obvious and most intimate of manifestations of the Goddess. After a few moments of contemplation, I decided to practice that enjoyable art of the ancients: meditative sleep. Many traditions seem to have embraced this technique – Taoists still diligently practise it, 'temple sleep' continues to be practiced in India, and in Greece there were at least three hundred temples dedicated to the healing god Aesculapius, at which those who required healing slept in special cells called *abatons*. The resulting sleep hopefully produced significant dreams, which were then interpreted by *therapeutes* (from whence our term 'therapeutic'). Such practices were also known to the ancient Druids. Wrapped in bull's hide, the Celtic seer would lie near a waterfall or spring, hoping for a dream of value. To determine the next High King in Ireland, the Druids would use similar techniques.

John Matthews, in an article entitled 'Auguries, Dreams and Incubatory Sleep among the Celts of Britain & Ireland', expands on Sir Mortimer Wheeler's suggestion that the Romano-British temple discovered at Lydney in Gloucestershire was in fact designed as a healing temple, complete with *abatons* to help incubate healing dreams. The evocative and healing powers of such places in Britain are now being explored by modern-day researchers. Volunteers offer to sleep at sacred sites. During the night, after they have shown signs of dreaming, a researcher awakens them to record the details of their dream. It is hoped that when enough experiments have been undertaken, a significant pattern of experiences related to sites will emerge.

Having no bull's hide to hand, I made do with my jacket, and curled up beside the Goddess and beside the river.

If you drift into sleep with a purpose, with a part of your conscious mind searching for an answer, seeking a point beyond the veil of logic, it can sometimes happen that, on awakening, your consciousness returns with an insight, an image, a powerful dream.

There was a doorway. I remember that. And a heart beating. And I went through and there was light. And then it seemed that I slept forever. But then suddenly there was noise and a sort of banging sound and a wide river of blood and I saw a great tall figure pushing open two huge doors and the river poured out on to the plain and in the river there were tigers and deer and ferrets and antelopes, big clumsy buzzards and bright kingfishers. If the animals had gone into the ark in an orderly fashion, they tumbled out of this one in great disarray - there were two of some species, but dozens of others. There were ants and spiders galore, and some great woolly mammoths too, walking into the distance determined to become fossils. I woke up to the sound of a baby crying.

A couple with a baby were walking along the path looking at me, worried perhaps that I was mad - sleeping rough at such a time of year.

Whether or not this triangular wood has been there since the days of the original carving of the Long Man, it is undeniable that today, at the legendary place of the Long Man's mate, we find this great image of the Goddess written in the landscape itself. And even though the White Horse towards the summit of the hill was only carved recently, it can hardly be a coincidence that they chose this hillside to carve it on. There are hillsides everywhere here, but it is on this hill that they chose to carve the symbol of the Goddess - a horse. Perhaps there had for centuries or millennia been the image of a horse on this hillside. As the annual scouring was abandoned, the image would have slowly faded, as did the Long Man's. And those who made the recent carvings would have been consciously or unconsciously simply re-carving, re-drawing the image.

As well as being the goddess's emblem, the horse is one of the totem animals of the British Isles. From the royal household to the street corner we are obsessed with horses. On the Berkshire Downs, the White Horse of Uffington prances across the hillside, with that mysterious and powerful long barrow, Waylands Smithy, nearby. Abroad they will eat them, but here their flesh is taboo.

But although the horse is particularly revered in Britain, the cult of Epona, the horse-goddess, was found throughout Europe. The only written record of this deity is found in the work of the Pseudo-Plutarch, who said: 'A certain Phouloniuos Stellos who hated women, had intercourse with a mare. In time, she brought forth a beautiful maiden whom she named Epona, a goddess of horses.' This strange story reminds us of the bizarre custom of the investiture of a new king in Donegal, recorded, in the twelfth century, by Giraldus Cambrensis in his *Itinerary of Ireland.* The new monarch bathed in the broth of a white mare's flesh and drank of its liquor after having had public intercourse with the poor animal.

Whilst our modern minds and hearts rebel against such rites, they offer one of the clearest demonstrations of the Indo-European roots of our Celtic ancestors: for in India, the Vedic *asvamedha* ritual required the queen to simulate intercourse with a stallion soon after it had been sacrificially slain.

Hard as it for our modern consciousness to grasp the meaning of these acts, we know that the horse was a symbol of the land for the ancients. A sovereign uniting with a horse symbolised the union of the king or queen with the land itself. By sharing in both its sexuality and its death, it seems that the sovereign took within him or herself its very life.

We see this mysterious and close association between

the horse and sexuality and death in the fact that those manifestations of the Horse Goddess that are still with us in folk tradition, are displayed at the two gateways of the year that represent death and sexuality respectively: the Celtic fire-festivals of Samhuinn and Beltane. Hobby horses are ridden either in Maytime or else in the winter months from Samhuinn to the New Year. The Padstow and Minehead Hobby Horses both bring in the May, while the Hooden Horse of Kent, and the Wild Horses of Cheshire and Shropshire, and the Mari Lwyd of South Wales usher in the Winter.

Psychoanalysis reveals that a horse can symbolise a person's libido or sexuality, but bad dreams of death and calamity are called nightmares, and it is said that death rides a pale horse.

The gates of life which on opening at Beltane allow in a great flood of ebullient energy which makes men feel like stallions and makes women refer to them as 'studs', on closing at Samhuinn carry that same force back into the Underworld, back to the Summer Isles to be renewed again through the Winter of this world...

Lucie

And as they were sitting down, they could see a lady on a big fine pale white horse, with a garment of shining brocaded silk upon her, coming along the highway that led past the mound. The horse had a slow even pace...and was coming level with the mound. 'Men,' said Pwyll, 'is there any among you who knows the rider?' 'There is not, lord,' said they.

'Pwyll Prince of Dyfed', The Mabinogion

Gathering up my jacket and rucksack I climbed up the steep path beside the triangle of woodland to be seated at last just above the white horse, looking down on the winding Cuckmere below. The sun came out, and in the warmth it was easy to drift back into the world of the Mother - the world of great gates opening to let the children and animals of earth tumble into the brightness of day. As I thought of my dream, of the animals and birds cascading through the great doorway of flesh in a river of blood, I realised that the Snake River does indeed, in our day, lead to a collection of diverse species - for just by Alfriston is one of the best small zoos in England at Drusillas. There flamingoes and otters, llamas and goats observe with disinterest their human spectators.

Amused by this pleasant conjunction of the archetypal and the actual, I realised how important it must have been for our ancestors to have had a river so close to their goddess hillside. From Mór, the Great Mother of the Sea, by the Seven Sisters, the grey waters flow past the goddess shrine towards the god at Windover, and beyond to Anderida - the Waste of Ondred.

But as I laid back, thinking of river and sea and goddess, I entered a state of reverie, and the Mother showed her other face to me: the brightness of day became the darkness of earth, the earth-belly initiation chamber became the barrow and passage-grave, the cries of the new-born became the cries of the dying. Her face was no longer the face of the loving mother and wife, but of the wrinkled and time-worn hag. 'I am both the giver and taker of life,' she said. 'This is the greatest mystery of all. You know of the joy and beauty that I bring to your life, but you know little of the sorrow and weeping. I know why life on earth must be given and taken - but you do not, and while you live on earth you will never fully know.' I opened my eyes, and tried, with little success, to shake off the sense of despair that had entered into me.

I walked on, along the Comp Track by Cradle Hill - marvelling at its great smooth sweep that was home to only a handful of sheep and a lone farmhouse. Choosing not the Green Way, but the track which runs via Norton Top and the tumulus of Five Lord's Burgh, I was soon high up on the Downs - with views of the sea and cliffs way behind and the lowering sun to the west. By early evening I was in Firle, seated in the pub which I had managed to avoid on the outward journey.

That night, at home, the telephone rang. The voice at the other end of the line seemed very far away. 'Lucie has been killed,' was all I heard.

As her mother continued to speak all I could hear was this one sentence repeating itself over and over again.

Lucie was seventeen. That morning she had driven with four other girls to have a picnic near the stables where they all worked. The car had crashed, the four other girls had survived, Lucie had not.

Every parent from the moment their child is born lives with a nightmare. Most of the time it never haunts us, even though each week we see the faces of parents on the television for whom the nightmare has come true: in Mogadishu, in Sarajevo, in Ulster.

Here on the telephone, that night, was a close friend who was living through that nightmare.

The horse which had carried Lucie each day through the country lanes and village streets of the Ribble Valley had become a pale terrifying horse that had bolted with her to another country far away. And we couldn't reach her.

Walking to the Tump immediately after the phone call, with her mother's words still echoing in my head, half disbelieving, half inwardly knowing, I was soon up on the summit. I could see the moon and the stars. I kneeled on the earth and put my face on the ground. Praying to the Mother of All Beings, I asked that Lucie might be granted a safe journey to the Isles of the Blessed. Standing up, I spoke to Lucie as if she were there, saying 'You are loved, you are blessed' over and over. Whereas three months previously it had seemed right just to pray and commune quietly for Boris, the friend who on the winter solstice had drifted gently out of this life at the age of 92, now it seemed important to do more. With the freedom from inhibition that shock and sorrow and being unobserved brings, I walked from north to west to south and then to east, asking out loud for the blessing of the spirits of each of the quarters for Lucie. I then found myself walking directly through the circle from east to west, standing facing outwards towards the quarter of the setting sun, of evening, of autumn, of departure. I cut through the circle that symbolises the cycle of our lives, to face the world beyond linear time, the Otherworld of Death.

Facing west to the Isles of the Blessed, and wishing Lucie well, I finished the ceremony.

That night, as I went to sleep, I sensed Lucie's presence close by. 'How are you?' I asked. She told me that she was 'okay', but that it had all been a bit of a shock to her. We talked about the journey that lay ahead, and about how all she needed to do was to feel herself travelling towards the Light. After a while she said goodbye, and with a little smile added 'Tell Mum not to sell my riding boots.' As I lay in bed, I thought 'What a strange thing to say...' But then I remembered - when she was tiny she had needed special orthopaedic shoes, and her parents had kept the little red boots as mementoes. They were her first shoes - the riding boots were her last - in this life.

The next day her mother asked if I would perform the funeral service at the crematorium. We then both remembered that she and Lucie's dad had performed the naming ceremony for our daughter, Sophie, on Iona two years previously. They had greeted our daughter as she entered the world - I was being asked to help us all wish their daughter well as she left our world. For hours the apparent injustice of this awful symmetry crashed into me in great waves of despair. Finally that strange calm that comes after a great deal of crying settled and stayed long enough for the realisation to dawn that in reality the two ceremonies are not that different.

In a Naming Ceremony, or baptism, we are recognising the safe arrival of a soul who has recently walked through the gateway from one world into another. In a funeral, or Parting Ceremony, we are asking for the safe arrival of a soul who has also recently walked through the gateway, although in the opposite direction: from this world to the next. It is even said that in the old days, some Celtic groups reversed their approach to these events: celebrating the birth of a soul into the Otherworld on their physical death, and mourning their death from the Otherworld on their physical birth.

Our knowledge of the after-death state which comes from all spiritual traditions, but in particular the Celtic, Egyptian and Tibetan, combined with the information we have gained through spiritualism, and now near-death studies, tells us that in a very real sense, death on the physical plane is indeed a birth into the spiritual world. Near-death studies consistently show the parallels: with the soul journeying through a dark tunnel towards the light, just as a baby struggles through a dark tunnel into the light of the world. For this reason, a Parting Ceremony needs to be a celebration of the new life that the soul has been born into and a celebration of their time on earth - all the while recognising and respecting the fact that this new step in the journey of the soul brings us great personal sadness.

Lucie's mother and father knew this. And despite their own sense of despair and tragedy, they knew too that in the Parting Ceremony we all needed to let Lucie go - to let her go on to the next stage of her journey. 'We want the ceremony to be a celebration of Lucie's life,' her father told me.

A little after the spring equinox, the day before Good Friday, on a clear and bright spring morning we gathered to say farewell.

Standing together with Lucie's mother and father on the seashore of Iona three weeks after her death, we talked of Lucie and of the journey that we are all taking through life. We talked of how death seems an initiation not only for the one who walks through the gateway, but also for those who must remain on this side of the threshold. We talked of how Lucie's step into the Other World had affected so many of us in ways we could never have imagined. Cairis and Will knew that although their tragedy was highly personal it was a tragedy that countless others must endure each year. Worldwide a quarter of a million people are killed by cars each year, in Britain four thousand people die annually as a result of car accidents. Whether by car or by age, by illness, accident or act of malice each of us will step through that doorway - and in stepping through we will leave our loved ones shocked and numbed. The way in which we honour the passing of our children or parents, our friends or relatives affects not only the journey of the departed one in the Otherworld, but also the journey in this world of those who are left behind.

That day in Scotland, gazing across the Sound of Iona to the snow-capped mountains of Mull on the farther shore, we agreed that it was important to share with others the ceremony that was used to honour Lucie's step into the Otherworld.

Lucie's Ceremony

O Great Spirit, mother and father of us all, we ask for your blessing on this our ceremony of thanksgiving and honouring and blessing of Lucie.

We stand at a gateway now, a gateway that each of us must step through at some time in our lives. Lucie has stepped through this gateway already. Her soul is immersed in the shining light of the Unity that is the mother and father of us all.

The sadness and the pain that we feel now is in our knowledge and our experience of the fact that we ourselves cannot yet cross that threshold to be with her until our time has come - until we too can begin what has been described as the Great Adventure.

Because Lucie was so young, and because her stepping through that gateway has been so sudden, there are many things that we wish now that we could have said to her, could have given her - many things that we wished for her and hoped for her. Lucie loved the song that we will hear now - and it speaks exactly of this, and as we listen to it, we can allow ourselves to feel and to communicate to her all that fills our hearts.

Music ('This Woman's Work' by Kate Bush)

Even though Lucie has begun the Great Adventure earlier, much earlier, than any of us could have imagined, we can come to understand now how each life on earth is complete in itself. Its very transience renders it beautiful. And we recognise and honour and respect and celebrate the beauty and the transience of Lucie's life here on earth.

Lucie loved adventure - she was a free spirit who abhorred the limitations of convention and conformity. She loved above all the world of nature and of animals. Her greatest pleasure was to ride her horse out into the country - free from the noise and the ugliness of towns and cars - close to the sun and the wind and the rain.

This world of nature that she loved so much is not confined to the reality that we experience here - it is one great continuous field of life, and religion after religion, and now scientific study after scientific study, shows us that life is not interrupted by physical death, but simply undergoes transition. Physical death is in fact for the person experiencing it, a birth - a freeing of the Self from the limitations of the body so that the soul can grow and learn and move in a brighter world - a world filled with light and depth, meaning and splendour. Lucie is in this world now and we can all join with her in celebrating and giving thanks for her time on this earth, thanks for the joy and laughter and love which she experienced and which she gave.

Let us have a moment of silence in which we each, in our own way, give thanks to Lucie for all that she gave us.

O Great Mother of all Being, we give thanks for what is given, we give thanks for what is taken. Even though we do not understand. Even though we do not understand.

Pelagius, a British theologian, who was probably a Druid, introduced in the fourth century the doctrine of Original Blessing, which states that each of us is born and dies blessed by God. To believe in this doctrine all we have to do is look into the eyes of a small child, all we had to do was look into Lucie's eyes. That was what struck me most about Lucie - the way her eyes were always sparkling. It seemed as if she perceived some great joke about the world that I hadn't quite understood... and it was utterly infectious: she made me laugh and smile even when I didn't know why. When she stayed with us last summer she regaled us with stories about her brother and her mum and dad that were full of a mischievous delight in the little sillinesses that we all display, but as she told us these stories, she knew and we knew, that she was really telling us how much she loved them - and how much she delighted in the quality that epitomises them - their humanity.

There is something that I would like to say to Cairis and Will that I know they know, but which nevertheless needs to be said: the pain and sorrow that we all feel today is in knowing that you are suffering the greatest wounding that can ever befall a man or woman on this earth. We know that and we stand with you now and we will always stand with you.

In Druid ceremonies, at certain moments, we stand and hold hands in a circle and say these words:

We swear by peace and love to stand, heart to heart and hand in hand.
Mark O Spirit and hear us now, Confirming this our sacred vow.

Take heart, take courage, and know that we cherish and love you.

In the great circle of life, we hold hands with more than just our present-day physical companions - we hold hands with the spirits of the animals and the trees, the stones and the stars - and we hold hands with all those we love on every plane of being.

Cairis and Will and Nolan, Lucie is not with you now in her body, but she will always be with you in Spirit. She lives in your hearts as you live in hers.

For there is no separation.

In one sense she is taking a long journey, the Great Adventure, riding her white horse to the Summer Isles, the Isles of the Blessed. But in another sense we know that the Great journey does not lead far away, but instead leads closer in: to the centre which unites us all.

Dear Lucie, may your journey to the Isles of the Blessed, to the centre of God/dess, to the land of freedom and splendour, be swift and sure. May your horse carry you with the wings of the Sun-God, may your stirrups hold you sure on the back of your steed. You are blessed, you are blessed, you are blessed. You are pure, you are pure, you are pure. Your purity is the purity of the divinity of the Holy Temple, therefore no evil shall befall you.

We ask that you might be guided by the name your mother and father gave you - for Lucie means Light. May the Light be your guide on the journey.

We ask that the blessing of the Spirits of the Tribe and of the Ancestors, of Time and of Place and of the Journey be with you.

We ask that the blessing of the Spirits of North and South, East and West be with you. We ask that you might be blessed with Fire and with Water, with Earth and with Air and with Spirit.

We ask for the blessing of the Lord and Lady of the Animals and the Woods, the Mountains and the Streams.

We ask that the blessing of the Uncreated One, whose child is the Created Word, and of the Spirit that is the Inspirer, may be always with you.

And in silence now we send Lucie our own blessings for a safe and joyous life in the Other World - filled with peace and clarity and love.

By the beauty of the fields, the woods and the sea, by the splendour that is set upon all that is, we send you our own love and blessings, dear Lucie.

As the sun rises in the East and sets in the West, so too are each of us born and so too do each of us die. But as the sun returns anew each day, so too do we return to earth, refreshed and renewed. Dear Lucie, know that just as you have been born into the spiritual world, so too will you be born again on earth - when it is right, in your own time. Now go safely, go well, go surely. Our hearts are with you. There is no separation.

Fare Thee well, Lucie.

Music ('On Your Shore' by Enya).

Rhiannon

The maiden stayed and waited, and drew back that part of her head-dress which should be over her face, and fixed her gaze upon him, and began to converse with him... 'Lady,' said he, 'wilt thou tell me anything of thine errands?' 'I will, between me and God,' said she. 'My main errand was to try to see thee.'

'Pwyll Prince of Dyfed', The Mabinogion

See Rhiannon as a richly-appointed queen with dark hair or else as a horse-headed woman with a foal at her side. She is the patron of all mothers who have suffered miscarriages or who have lost their children in an untimely fashion.

from the teaching material of the Druid Grade of The Order of Bards Ovates & Druids

It was impossible to continue the journey. Just as the circle on the Mound that night had been cleaved in two by walking directly through it from east to west, so too had the journey from the Mound and back to it again via Wilmington been cleaved in two by Lucie's death.

But the old tales give us support in times of despair - this is one of the great values of myth and story. The story of Christ's life and his crucifixion has provided this support to some for generations, but for many of us we need to look further back, deeper into our heritage - closer than the Middle East, nearer than the shores of Galilee or the Mount of Olives.

One of the great sources of inspiration for the Druidic and Celtic mythos is to be found in that collection of magical Welsh tales known as the Mabinogion. Although not actually set down in writing until the twelfth century, it is clear that the stories of the Mabinogion draw on pre-Christian sources.

The first of the tales, known as the 'first branch' of the Mabinogion is entitled *Pwyll Prince of Dyfed* and tells of the prince's marriage to a woman from the Otherworld - Rhiannon - and of the mysterious disappearance and reappearance of their son - Pryderi.

Having spent a year and a day in the Underworld, the Prince decided to seat himself on the Mound of Arberth, a magical mound that either wounds or shows a wonder to those of nobility who dare to climb it: 'Pwyll arose to take a walk, and made for the top of a mound which was above the court and was called Gorsedd Arberth. 'Lord,' said one of the court, 'it is the peculiarity of the mound that whatever high-born man sits upon it will not go thence without one of two things: wounds or blows, or else his seeing a wonder.'

Sitting upon the mound, he sees 'a lady on a big fine pale white horse...coming along the highway that led past the mound.' A rider is sent to intercept her, and although her horse keeps a slow steady pace, the rider fails to reach her. This occurs three times. Finally, Pwyll rides towards her and calls out to her to stop. This she does, saying, 'I will gladly, and it had been better for the horse hadst thou asked this long since.' It can take some men a long time to understand that women need words as well as action.

She reveals to Pwyll that she loves only him, although she has been betrothed against her will to another man. She invites him to her father's hall in a year and a day to outwit her unwanted husband. This done, they sleep together and return to Dyfed to rule together until Rhiannon bears a son. Although they wait for over three years to have their first-born, on the evening of his birth the baby is plucked mysteriously from his cradle as his mother and her six maids sleep.

When the maids wake up they are terrified that they will be blamed for the child's disappearance. They kill a puppy and smear its blood on Rhiannon's face and mouth as she sleeps. They leave a few of its bones on her bed. When she awakes she asks: 'Women, where is the child?' 'Lady,' said they, 'ask not us for the child. We are nothing but blows and bruises from struggling with thee...Thou hast thyself destroyed thy son.'

Pwyll stands by his wife, despite the public outrage. 'So Rhiannon summoned to her teachers and wise men. And as she preferred doing penance to wrangling with the women she took on her her penance.' And her penance was to sit every day for seven years by a mounting block outside the gate at the court of Arberth. To each visitor she had to recount the whole story and then offer to carry them on her back into the court.

Not only must she suffer the sorrow of the loss of her child, but she must each day proclaim the lie that she has taken its life, and become a horse that carries each visitor to court.

But the deeper our sorrow, the harsher the injustice and indignity we must face, the greater will be our reward - in the end.

The time the baby had been snatched from his sleeping mother had been Beltane - May Eve. And in another part of the country a man called Teyrnon was preparing to discover why each year at Beltane he lost the foal that was born to his mare. He decided to stand guard over her that very night. As the foal was born, a monstrous claw came through the window to steal it, but Teyrnon swiftly struck at the clawed arm with his sword, severing it with one blow. There was a scream and a commotion and he rushed outside in pursuit of the monster. In the pitch black of the night he could see nothing, and then he remembered that he had left the door open. He ran back inside to discover 'an infant boy in swaddling clothes, with a sheet of brocaded silk wrapped around him.'

Terynon and his wife raised the boy, calling him Gwri Golden-hair. By the time he was two, he was as big as a six year-old.

Hearing of the sad news of Rhiannon and her penance, Terynon realised that Gwri looked remarkably like Pwyll: 'And with that, anxiety seized upon him, so very wrong it was for him to keep the boy when he knew him to be another man's son. And the first time he had privacy with his wife, he told her it was not right for them to keep the boy with them, and allow such great punishment as was for that reason on so excellent a lady as Rhiannon.'

The next day Teymon and Gwri rode to Arberth. Rhiannon met them as they drew near the court, saying 'Chieftain, go no further than that; I will carry each one of you to the court, and that is my penance for killing my son with my own hands and destroying him.'

They refused to be carried and announced instead the news of her son's return to the assembled company in the court. Amidst great rejoicing the boy was renamed Pryderi and Terynon was offered 'the fairest jewels and the finest horses and choicest dogs; but not a thing would he have.'

This story proclaims the enduring truth that we can never be truly separated from those we love. In time we are reunited - and the length of time that seemed to separate us vanishes in a moment. Those of us who are separated from our children through death or divorce or other circumstance can hold fast to the knowledge that our sense of separation is only temporary - and at the deepest level it is illusory even though it cuts us to the quick. Rhiannon the Otherworldly

Queen is doubly wounded - by loss and by false accusation. She knows the truth and she waits for the Time of Return. She stands in her dignity and majesty and integrity as a goddess to whom all those who have been falsely accused, or from whom children have been taken, can turn for succour and support.

Rhiannon and Pwyll travel to and fro between this world and the Otherworld. For most of us this travel is not so easy, and it is only on death that we find ourselves entering the Otherworld. Part of the training of the Mystery Schools, including that of the Druids, involves acquiring an ability to voyage to some degree into these realms without having to physically die each time we make a voyage. Even so, the sorrow we experience when someone close to us dies comes from knowing that they have begun a journey on which we cannot accompany them, however much we may have become familiar with the Otherworld through meditation or inner journeying. But death, like life, is full of paradoxes and although in one sense, on experiencing death of the body we begin a new stage of our journey, becoming a traveller in a wider brighter world, in another sense we may well discover that there is no journey - only a continuing revelation of the still centre - God/dess - the heart of Being. We uncover a great truth when we realise we are on a journey through life. We uncover a great truth when we realise there is no journey.

> We shall not cease from exploration
> And the end of all our exploring
> Will be to arrive where we started
> And know the place for the first time.
> Through the unknown, remembered gate
> When the last of earth left to discover
> Is that which was the beginning;
> At the source of the longest river
> The voice of the hidden waterfall

And the children in the apple-tree
Not known, because not looked for
But heard, half-heard, in the stillness
Between two waves of the sea.

T.S.Eliot

The Journey Home

I saw the tower in the woods, and flowering thistles
in the lush lanes, and the earnest war-felled timber,
and perceived a faith that burned in slow mouths of the folk
under their conscious thinkings and repeated formulae:
the old lines of knowledge continuing, life surely renews;
the final objective not knowing, we still are content.
I plead very guilty to being indeed my own ancestor.

Nuinn

Lucie had died on 10 April - a little after the spring equinox. By Beltane we were on Iona celebrating May Day with a fire beside the sea-shore, the sound of the crashing waves and the crackling flames meeting in our consciousness as we closed our eyes beside the fire. After Lucie's death I couldn't complete the journey and I couldn't write. Coming back from Iona I thought I could begin again - when beginning again meant actually finishing the walk and completing this book. The final part of the journey was, after all, only the five miles that separates Firle from Lewes. But those five miles seemed to represent an infinite distance - an eternity of time.

On 10 June our second daughter was born - with all the wonder and joy that a new baby brings into the world. On 21 June we celebrated the summer solstice, known in the Druid tradition as Alban Hefin, The Light of the Shore, on Primrose Hill in London. Two hundred years previously Druids from Wales and England had gathered here through the invitation of the Welsh bard Iolo Morganwg. Now, at the bicentennial celebrations, Druids from Wales and England, Ireland, Scotland, Brittany and France, America and Australia, Finland, Hungary and Holland gathered on that same sacred hill to celebrate not only the memory of that historic moment of the Druid Revival two hundred years ago, but also the fact that in these closing years of the second millennium, Druidry is experiencing a revival not just in the traditionally Druidic lands but worldwide. We wanted to honour the contribution of Druids both past and present, and so Lucie's mother Cairisthea fashioned a ceremony that combined aspects of the traditional rite, which draws to a great extent on Iolo's work, with her own inspired wording and ritual choreography.

At the high point of the ceremony, a couple who had been married at a Druid wedding at Imbolc walked to the centre of the circle to join hands. They spoke for Love. The Scribe then asked 'Who will speak for the Land?' From around the circle came the reply: 'We will speak for the Land,' and from out of the circle stepped representatives from each of the many countries present - joining hands in a smaller inner circle surrounding the central couple. Those left in the original ceremonial circle spoke for the People of these Lands, and the guardians of each quarter spoke for Peace. As Chief in the ceremony, I then said: 'On this day of greatest light we stand in celebration, three in one: Love, the Lands, and the People, encircled by Peace. May the Sun that is the inspirer shine within our hearts that we may go from this place knowing that we live as One People on the One Earth that is our home.'

All seemed complete. But the Herald called out 'There is another who wishes to enter our fellowship. The Mabon asks that we may hear him.' The Mabon, as representative of the Divine Child, then penetrated from the outer circle to the centre of the three circles, holding aloft a light and saying 'I come to this place as a child of future generations. My gift is the gentle flame of hope that each new life brings into the world. I and those who follow me, ask that those of you who speak for Love, the Lands and the People, protect this Sacred Flame. You who are the earthly guardians of wisdom unite together in peace and harmony to protect this planet, our home. This I ask for the children of the world.'

Here was the focus of the Druid revival today - not on the past, despite its splendour and its richness of heritage, but on the future: on the need for us to preserve this beautiful planet for our children. The call of Druidry today is a call from the future, even though it is a call rooted in the past and in the authority of tradition. Like a great tree it has roots that stretch far back in time - to our primal pre-Celtic origins, perhaps even to Atlantis. And because it is so well rooted it means that its branches stretch high up into the air and its fruit are plentiful. In truth there is no separation in time as there is no separation in space: The songs of our ancestors are also the songs of our children. It is the pure haunting song of our children that we hear now as we gaze out upon our world knowing that it is our generation - no other - that must cease its destruction.

After the summer solstice ceremony I could begin again - finishing the journey that had started exactly six months previously at the Tump on the winter solstice. But it was another seven weeks before the time was right. On 1 August my wife Stephanie drove me to The Ram at Firle, and as the car swept away I was alone again, with just a back-pack and a map. This time there would be no rendezvous - I would walk home having crossed the final range of the Downs that separates Firle from Lewes.

Walking behind the pub and then across open fields I felt again that extraordinary sense of freedom that comes when you set off alone on foot across the land. The other stages of the journey had taken place in winter, then in early spring -

now it was the height of summer. Leaving Firle and heading towards Glynde you would think from the map that the road separating these two villages would destroy all sense of being in the open countryside, but as I walked beside the wide fields of waving waist-high corn I could neither see nor hear the road. Instead I saw to my left the long height of the South Downs Way, with Firle beacon to the east and Itford Hill to the west. Ahead lay Swanborough Hill capped with menacing dark clouds, and to my right was Mount Caburn bathed in sunshine and beckoning me towards it. Stopping to admire the view, I knelt down so that the waving corn became a golden sea, with the Dun before me a great green boat. At the prow stood the Firle Giant on his beacon laughing and throwing small flat stones that skipped across the wheat sea towards me. At the ship's bridge, the two radio masts of Beddingham Hill rose like the two staves of the Long Man thrust into the ground as a symbol of balance and communication.

As the giant's boat sailed from the Isis to Snake River, I turned around, just in time to find the Gill Giant of Mount Caburn gazing out from his hill-top fort. When he saw me, he raised his right arm and hurled a huge hammer that spun and circled in the air before landing with a crash in the wheat beside me. I ran over to it and picked it up. As I held it, I found it was not a hammer but an axe. I remembered that axes were often used as sacred objects and were buried beneath tracks. Thanking the giant, I used the axe to dig a hole beneath the path - burying it like the man who buried the chalk phallus on Itford Hill, like a dog burying a bone knowing it will be dug up one day.

As I walked on, I remembered Brian Bates' tale of an Anglo-Saxon sorcerer, *The Way of Wyrd*, that is set in ancient Sussex. Dr Bates, Senior Lecturer in psychology and head of the Shaman Project at Sussex University, had unearthed in the British Museum a thousand-year-old manuscript from the Anglo-Saxon period. In this manuscript were recorded the magico-medical techniques of pagan sorcerers, including herbal remedies, rituals, incantations and spells. Rather than writing about the manuscript academically, Dr Bates chose to weave the material he had discovered into an imaginary story about the experiences of Wat Brand, a Christian scribe who became apprenticed to a sorcerer called Wulf.

In referring to the way in which ancient beliefs can complement our understanding of medicine, healing, ecology and personal transformation, Dr Bates believes that a study of our own heritage, as well as that of the East can provide valuable insights and can offer 'teachings, concepts, perspectives and experiences that speak to us with a provocative and compelling relevance to contemporary existence.' His book deals specifically with the theories and practices of Anglo-Saxon sorcery, which derive their inspiration mainly from Nordic mythology. But the Tree of Tradition in these islands has many roots: from where we stand now, the Celtic and pre-Celtic, the Megalithic, Christian and the Nordic roots all weave together to feed the central trunk that is the Matter of Britain - the heritage of spiritual practices and beliefs that is so massive we have hardly touched its surface. Earlier in my life I felt as if it was only in other cultures that there was a vast reservoir of authentic spiritual practice and tradition. It seemed as if the Indian, Tibetan or Native American cultures were perhaps the only guardians of truly genuine or intact lines of ancient spirituality. Now, the more I learn the more I realise that in reality we are sitting on such a reservoir of spiritual tradition in Britain that it is impossible for one individual to fully articulate the richness of this heritage. As an example: in 1992, of the manuscripts relating to Druidry and the Celtic Tradition in Ireland only one quarter have been translated into English. The rest – 75 per cent of the records of this heritage - remain untranslated in libraries in Ireland and Switzerland.

The Megalithic and pre-Celtic, Celtic, Roman, Nordic and Saxon traditions met and mingled, were changed and transformed. So when Wulf, the Anglo-Saxon sorcerer in *The Way of Wyrd* roams these same hills and valleys, his understanding of the hidden forces must be very close to that of the Druids who lived here and walked these tracks before him.

Within this small portion of Logres between the Waste of Ondred and the sea we find traces of four great giants - the giants of Firle and of Hunter's Burgh, where now stands the Long Man, the Gill giant on Mount Caburn, and the Nameless Giant in Lewes itself. The Gill giant now lies buried in Gill's Grave - a barrow near Glynde, and it was the Nameless Giant of Lewes who was responsible for hollowing out the great coombe in the Downs behind the town.

Wulf explains who these giants are to his Christian friend, Brand, in this way:

> The giants are the gods of old. The world was made from giants, in the first winter. A mighty giant was created from hoarfrost. And when fire came, he melted. From the enormous bulk of his body came the worlds. From his blood flowed the sea, from his bones the mountains, from his hair the forests, from his skull the sky. And from his lashes, covering the eyes that beheld all, was fashioned Middle-Earth, land of people, sorcerers and spirits. In the centre of Middle-Earth, on hills rising high as mountains, live the gods, and below seethes the Underworld, land of the dead and all their secrets... [But] the giants are now outcasts, living as exiles on the fringe of the earth, kept at bay by a mighty ocean surrounding Middle-Earth.

So the giants I had seen were not really there - they were ghosts of giants, echoes from another time, a time before windmills and cars, before radio masts and satellites. Or were they? Just as we humans die only in order to be born again at a later time, perhaps the giants too will return to uproot the roads and railway tracks, the factories and rocket silos that we have littered across the earth.

But why exactly are giants so prevalent in folklore and myth? It has been suggested that stories of giants reflect memories of real physical giants, freaks perhaps or taller races. At a psychological level the image of the giant or giantess is explicable in terms of the infant's experience of adults: we are truly giants to our children as we scoop them up from knee height to sit them on our shoulders or carry them through busy streets thronging with other giants. We can even understand the theme of the Lonely Giant in terms of the peculiarly masculine alienation and loneliness that emanates from the psychologically or physically absent father: imagine the feelings of a sailor's child when daddy returns from months away at sea, months which feel to the child like years. This maybe bearded and gruff near-stranger, disconnected through absence and culture from his own family, might carry his child on his shoulders or in his arms for a while until the day he again returns to sea, leaving the child with memories of warmth and sadness - of loneliness for both the child and the giant who might or might not return one day.

Whilst this explanation may be partly satisfying, it cannot fully explain the prevalence of giants in myth. There is, however, a further level of psychological explanation: instead of looking outside, we look within, and we see the giants in ourselves. When sexual or combative power flows through us we act as if we are greater than our normal selves - physically larger and stronger. The Amazon was often seen as a giantess if not in size then in strength: she epitomised the power of sexuality and the warrior. On Britain's farthest-flung island, St Kilda, whose first Christian missionary arrived in 1705, Stallir the Druid and a Druidess known as the Amazon lived. She adored hunting, and set her hounds to chase the deer across to Harris and Lewis, since back then there was dry land between St.Kilda and the Outer Hebrides. The combination of overt sexual power and the warrior spirit in the male are graphically portrayed by the Cerne Abbas Giant's raised penis and club. When we encounter within us the Wild Man or Woman (or indeed many archetypal parts of ourselves) it can often feel as if we are larger, bigger, stronger than our everyday selves.

But clearly there is still more to this giant business. If we look above we see the figures of giants marked in the heavenly constellations, and when they become angry they hurl rocks which thud to the earth as meteorites. If we look around us we see giants in the landscape: rockfaces that look like huge heads, mountain horizons that are like the profiles of giants lazing on their backs, curving slopes that echo the forms of breasts and thighs and pregnant bellies. On Cliffe Hill by Lewes, from the garden allotments that lie between great thighs of land, your eye is led towards a wooded cleft and then up the belly of the hill to the two breasts called the Camel's Humps - two barrows that neolithic man may well have placed to aesthetically and geomantically complete the picture nature had so generously made. And showing that such ideas are not the product of modern minds obsessed with the body and sexuality, the old folk who work the allotments remember that the hill had always been called 'The Fat-bellied Woman' and that it was no accident that the soil was so fertile.

Whilst it can be argued that we see giant figures in the landscape just as we might determine figures from the fire or clouds, it is possible that a deeper mystery is here: some researchers have found that certain parts of the landscape possess chakra systems, series of seven different energy vortices, in the same way that the human body has a series of such centres. Instead of our projecting notions of a mighty being outwards from ourselves to the 'blank screen' of Nature, we may sometimes actually be in the presence of mighty beings who are not projections or fantasies of ours at all.

If giants and giantesses represent not only the land personified but something more - the living nature of the landscape - then no wonder that great heights or landscape formations often have an associated giant or giantess legend: hence the giants of hills such as Firle in Sussex or Pendle in Lancashire, for example, or the rock formations known as the Giantess' Apron in Wales or the Giant's Causeway in Ireland.

When the giants are drawn in the chalk itself, we have the most potent representation of the meeting of the Sky Father with the Earth Mother. The chalk hill figures become then symbols of the union of the gods. By carving the giant figures of Cerne Abbas or Wilmington into Mother Earth, our ancestors were literally, with their hands, fusing together the Sky or Sun God with his consort the land - there was no more separation: god and goddess were one.

But there is yet one more level of explanation. This tells of other planes of being, of other worlds: of the Inner Planes, or 'Non-Ordinary Reality' as some researchers now prosaically term these realms of existence. It is here that giants and giantesses may truly and objectively exist - it is here that we meet the mighty beings whom we term devas or angels, gods or goddesses, giants or giantesses. And it is these beings, glimpsed at special places of power, and embodying vast reserves of elemental force, who over time may have become depicted in rhyme and song, in dance and carnival, as the giants of fairy-tale.

Turning from the track for a brief moment I crossed the road that runs from Lewes to Eastbourne to walk towards Glynde - towards the Gill giant's home.

The Slopes of the Galedin

A slumberous silence of abundant light, of the full summer day, of the high flood of summer hours whose tide can rise no higher...a time to linger and dream... As I move about in the sunshine I feel in the midst of the supernatural; in the midst of immortal things... I am a pagan, and I think the heart and soul above crowns.

Richard Jefferies,
The Story of My Heart

Walking from Firle to Glynde you walk from one feudal village to another - Lord Gage owns most of Firle and Lord Hampden owns most of Glynde... and here at Glynde every summer thousands of immaculately dressed people descend by car or train or helicopter to visit one of the most famous opera-houses in the world at Glyndebourne. Few realise that close to the lake and gardens which play host to the world's opera lovers, a giant lies sleeping in his barrow.

One day, beneath the song of the baritones and basses his booming voice will be heard again as he talks in his sleep of another time, when Middle Earth was still his home, and he could walk freely across the hills.

Resisting the temptation to visit the gardens of Glynde Place, I veered to the left and climbed the stile to begin the ascent to Mount Caburn.

The hillside was covered in poppies, bee orchids and rampion, and the dark clouds that had gathered earlier by Swanborough Hill suddenly swept overhead and within minutes I was thoroughly soaked. But also within minutes the rainclouds moved on, to be replaced by a clear blue sky and a brilliant midday sun.

After a while I reached the outer ramparts of Mount Caburn. Entering the gateway of mound and ditch, I came to the centre of this high and powerful place. Despite it being in the middle of summer, there was no-one there: not a soul in this ancient and beautiful spot. And then I just followed my instincts and took off my clothes and spun and danced around in the sunshine, then lay on the grass feeling its softness on my back, and the sun and gentle breeze on the front of my body. I sat up and was filled with a simple, clear feeling of joy, as if, like Horace Walpole, I had cast off my cares as I had cast off my clothes. I wondered for a moment whether I was mad or indeed legal – could I be arrested for simply being myself here? Was I somehow only legally entitled to exist if covered? Why was it so pleasing and more than that, why did it feel so important to be naked at this moment?

I remembered the grand tradition of Naturism – born out of a love of the sun, the fresh air and of Nature herself, and born too out of a struggle with the grey repressive forces of prudery and Puritanism. Nakedness means freedom, and although dancing on a sun-kissed hillside with shorts on seems pretty similar to dancing with shorts off, there is all the difference in the world. It is as if your clothes take on the weight of your worries and concerns – they come to embody your defences against the world, and if you can feel confident enough and safe enough, then taking them off evokes a powerful sense of liberation, of joy and freedom;

and more than that – of innocence and of openness to the world. That explained to me why I felt joyful and why I felt it important to do this. I was open to the world here, high on Mount Caburn. There was nothing between me and Nature. I felt at one with it.

I realised that this was why so many writers who loved Nature waxed lyrical about the joys of being naked outdoors: Richard Jefferies, Francis Kilvert, George Bernard Shaw, Edward Carpenter, Thoreau, Walt Whitman. They had all discovered the 'secret' that you don't need any thing to be happy. As if in an opposite process to consumerism, which feeds us the lie that only more things can make us happy, the minimalism of Naturism tells us that we don't even need clothes to find happiness. Less truly becomes more, and in this moment I found an even greater respect for the Naturism of my teacher Nuinn, and of his friend Gerald Gardner, who adopted the Jain term 'skyclad' as a poetic alternative to the starker term 'nude'.

After a while of skyclad meditation, listening to the lark song and soaking in the sunshine and the summer breeze, I dressed again, and walking to the edge of the outer henge, I understood why this is a favourite spot for hang-gliders. The Old People chose the places for their forts and settlements with care: not only were they sighted with regard to natural defences and accessibility of resources such as flint, food or water, but they were also clearly chosen with aesthetics in mind too. The sites of Mount Caburn or of Whitehawk (reached by walking along Jugg's Road towards Brighton) for example, are superbly sited with magnificent panoramas laid out before them.

There, straight ahead across the valley was Itford Hill, with the Brookland basin down to the right. I could just catch glimpses of the river Isis meandering her way towards the sea. But the city of Lugh itself was hidden from view by the last hill.

I turned to look at the green mounds behind me – the only traces that now remain of the earthwork fort that had been on this hill and that had been attacked by the Romans. I imagined the smoking remains of wooden buildings, and the debris of a long and bloody battle. But instead of blood there were tulips everywhere, and everywhere too was field flea-wort, a relative of the common ragwort, which is found in abundance for some strange reason, on ancient earthworks. Thousands of years may pass, but the wort flowers refuse to change their habits.

I thought back on the journey - a journey I had naively believed would take only a few days or weeks to complete, but which in reality had taken over seven months. And in those months so much had happened.

My destination was near, and yet still I couldn't see it. For much of the outward journey in February, Lewes had glowed in the sunshine - so that I could see it and the Tump even as I climbed Itford Hill, but almost all the way on the return journey it had been obscured by the terrain, as it was now, even though it was so close.

The hill that I was on had been home, originally, to an undefended farm established about 2,500 years ago. But in around 150 BCE defences were hastily created just before it was attacked, probably by invading Belgae. These tribespeople, having conquered the farm-fort, dug over one hundred granary pits, created what was probably a water storage tank, and strengthened the fortifications. Despite the extra ramparts, the fort was attacked and reduced to ashes - almost certainly by Roman troops. Despite its bloody end, the site today is one of great peace and beauty. Recent archaeological work at the site now suggests that the hill-top may also once have been a sacred site – evidence of ancient yews has been found, and it is possible that it was the site of a sacred grove, as was Lullington across the valley.

Leaving Mount Caburn, the footpath leads you down

a green motorway of the soul - a broad grassy slope with waving carnation sedge and broome to either side marking out the human traffic lane of this flowing hillside. And then it narrows past Bible Bottom, a strange square-shaped earthwork, to the golf course that crowns Cliffe Hill. Walking through the alien terrain of manicured lawns and metal flags leads you finally to the Western slope of Cliffe Hill from which, at last, Lewes is visible.

On Cliffe Hill neolithic farmers ploughed their terraced lynchets, and may well have inhabited the hill on which Lewes now stands. There is evidence that the churches of St.John sub Castro and St.Anne's occupy early pre-Christian ritual sites, and there are suggestions of Roman activity. But the most definite signs of settlement date from Anglo-Saxon times, when massive entrenchments were dug to fortify the town against Danish raids, probably before King Alfred's death in 899.

The origin of the name Lewes is popularly explained as deriving from the Old English *hlaew,* meaning a hill, but without further clarification this explanation is misleading. Most residents of Lewes probably believe that their town's name derives from the hill on which it is built. But Margaret Gelling, President of the English Place-Name Society, estimates that the word *hlaew* was very rarely if ever used in Southern England to describe a natural hill. Instead it was used to denote an artificial mound or tumulus. Dr Gelling believes Lewes is so-called because of the tumuli which dot the hills to the east and west of the town. But recent research by John Bleach of the Sussex Archaeological Society reveals evidence that shows there might have been at least seven mounds within the town itself, suggesting that the origin of the name may come not from the sacred mounds outside the town, but from those within it.

Standing on Cliffe Hill looking down on Lewes, you notice immediately - despite the accumulation of modern-day buildings - the three mounds of the Tump by the Priory ruins, the motte beneath Lewes Castle and Brack Mount, often described as the castle's second motte. John Bleach has uncovered records of a further four mounds near the church of St John sub Castro. If most or all of these mounds were in existence in Saxon times, then indeed this was a fitting place to be called by the Saxons *Hlaewes* - the Place of the Mounds.

The fact is that *hlaew* (and hence its derivations *lew* and *low*) was used not simply to denote any mound, but to denote a mound of importance: hence Mutlow in Cambridgeshire and Essex means 'Moot Mound', Knightlow Hill in Ryton means 'mount or tumulus of the young men', Brinklow probably means 'tumulus on the brink of a hill', and Pathlow in Aston Cantlow means 'mound or tumulus by the path.'

Harlow in Essex is named after a small hill by the railway station, which in ancient times was surmounted by a Roman temple. Artificially scarped and surrounded by a ditch, no doubt the Romans were not the first to sense its summit as sacred.

The name of Ludlow in Shropshire means 'mound by the torrent', or by other reckonings 'the mound of Lugh' (from Lud). In *The History of Ludlow*, T.Wright proposed yet another meaning for the town's name, and in the following quotation we find further clues to the importance of those names deriving from *hlaew*:

> [Ludlow] ...signifies the hill of the people. But the Anglo-Saxon *hlaew* was generally applied not to a natural hill like that on which the town of Ludlow [or indeed Lewes] stands, but to an artificial burial-mound, a tumulus or barrow, like the Bartlow Hills in Cambridgeshire... These lows were intimately connected with the mythology and superstitions of our early forefathers, and in their minds were wrapped up with the notions of primeval giants and

dragons which kept a jealous watch over their hidden treasures. In old times we find them frequently the scenes of popular ceremonies and meetings.

One of the three mounds of Lewes was almost certainly the focus of such popular ceremonies - the Tump at harvest time. And it is around the Tump that the dragon-path is coiled to protect its bright treasure. Perhaps the name Lewes honours this sacred site in particular.

And how fitting it would be if this city of the sacred mounds was chosen by the Knights Templar to shelter the Holy Grail, as local rumour suggests. The first Templar church in Britain was apparently in Albion Street in Lewes. This church of the Holy Sepulchre was visited by the head of the Templars Hugues de Payen.

The origin of the name Lewes has for years seemed anchored in the Old English *hlaew*. But recently, local place-name expert Richard Coates of Sussex University has suggested that it is equally possible that the name Lewes derives from the same root as the Welsh word *llechwedd,* meaning 'slope'. The source of *llechwedd* is *lexowia*, from the British - the Celtic language of Britain spoken until the departure of the Roman legions.

Lewes is indeed built on a slope, or a number of slopes as those who live in the town well know as they struggle up and downhill. And support for Dr. Coates' theory comes from an unlikely source - the bard responsible for the Welsh Druid revival Iolo Morganwg. It was Morganwg who initiated the Gorsedd of Bards on Primrose Hill in 1792, whose bicentennial we had commemorated that summer, and whose ceremonies form the basis of the Welsh Gorsedd to this day. But much to the embarrassment of the Welsh, a good deal of Iolo's writings have been found to emanate not - as he claimed - from original documents since lost, but from his own fertile imagination. However, a certain amount of the material he presented to the world may well be authentic. One of these fragments may well be the one entitled 'The Principal Territories of Britain'.

Iolo Morganwg claimed to have transcribed this from a manuscript in the possession of a Mr Cobb of Cardiff. Of the sixteen areas listed, all but one are known to historians. The one that remains obscure is the territory of *Arllechwedd Galedin*. But its borders are described in the text as certain of the principal British territories are listed:

> 13. Caint [Kent] - from the river Tain [Thames] and Mor Tawch [the Misty Sea] to the confines of Arllechwedd Galedin.
> 14. Arllechwedd Galedin - from the last territory to the extremities of Dyvnaint [Devon] Gwlad yr Hav [Somerset] and Argoed Calchvynydd [The hills of limestone or chalk by the forest].
> 15. Dyvnaint and Cerniw [Cornwall] from Arllechwedd Galedin and the intermediate seas, to the British Channel.

By marking out the boundaries as given in the manuscript, we discover that the territory described appears to be Sussex with part of Hampshire too.

Arllechwedd means 'The slopes of' and the *Galedin* have been referred to as 'the people who came from the land which was flooded'. How appropriate it would be if one of the principal cities of *Arllechwedd Galedin* had been called *Llechwedd*, later becoming known as Lewes. And how extraordinarily romantic it would be if we were to discover that the Galedin were a people fleeing from the flooded Atlantis, rather than the more likely explanation that they were Saxons fleeing from their flooded lowlands.

I was told about this reference to Sussex in the Iolo Manuscripts by a man whom I met on the top of the Tump one morning before the start of my journey. We talked about the Tump beneath us and the surrounding countryside.

Months later, as the journey came to an end, we met again, introduced this time by a mutual friend, and he told me of his discovery of this reference in Iolo's work. As the journey neared completion, it felt as if the Inner Name of this land could now be told - as if the dragon of the Tump had allowed one of its jewelled secrets to be known again.

And if you slept here on this land, tucked up in a warm bed that seemed anchored in the modern world, your consciousness might well slip free from the confines of linear time that limit your awareness. Then you would slide into the Past as easily as you might slide into a pool, and there you would be: on the slopes of the Galedin, seven sacred hills dominating the landscape. Beneath the fighting of Saxons, Danes, Belgae and Romans, of people before them and after them; beneath the rush of traffic, and of the planes flying high above on their way to Gatwick from Rome and Brussels and Copenhagen, there would the steady pulse of the earth, the breeze blowing inland from the sea, and the sight of seven hills catching the first rays of dawn on a new morning.

The Harvest

The longest way round is the shortest way home.

C.S. Lewis

Walking down from Cliffe Hill, I reached Chapel Hill that leads into Cliffe High Street. Suddenly there were the people I saw every day, and the shops that I knew so well, but I was approaching them from a different viewpoint. I was an outsider coming down from the hills. I was a walker not a shopper. My purpose was journeying not buying. But strangely, as I walked through the High Street, I felt that at last I had come home.

I crossed over Cliffe Bridge, whose medieval forebear had witnessed the miracle of St.Richard of Chichester, and turned into Friars Walk, making my way towards the beginning and the end of my journey.

By the time I reached the Tump it was early evening, but it was still warm. I climbed the dragon path, and for a while sat and gazed out at the view from the summit. I found myself wondering how such a small man-made hill could seem so essential, so magical - such a key to exploring the landscape. As if hearing my question, I found that Nuinn had appeared, seated beside me: ‘This hill, this Tump,’ he told me, ‘is a Lughnasadh Hill, a hill specially built by women and men thousands of years ago to commemorate this time at the beginning of August, when the god Lugh brings the crops to fruition and when it is time to gather in the harvest. Corn is sacred - look at the significance of bread in the Christian tradition - it is seen as the flesh of Christ. How can we deny his reality as a vegetation god when the symbolism is so clear? Whether we see bread as the body of Christ or as the offering of the body of the Mother Goddess it is undeniable that it is a gift of life to us.'

I remembered Maire MacNeill's study of this time of Lughnasadh, in which she showed that even as recently as the 1960's, Lughnasadh was being celebrated in Ireland on ninety-five hill-tops, by ten lakes and five river banks. In Scotland local communities built turf Lammas towers up until the eighteenth century, and even today conical Lammas cakes - like little tumps - are baked each year at this time. Here, and at Silbury Hill, and undoubtedly at other points in the vast network of shining trackways across the land, were built such Lammas towers that have survived as mounds to this day.

Nuinn began to speak again: 'No-one is really certain of the origin of this strange serpent-mound. Some say it was a Norman motte, or simply the spoil-heap created when the neighbouring medieval salt-pan was built. Others say it was a mound built over the horses killed in the Battle of Lewes in 1264, while still others think it was a Roman light-house, a look-out place for the castle, a calvary hill built by monks, or a viewing mound built as part of a renaissance water garden. But you and I and others too know that it was none of these things. It was built to celebrate the harvest, and it was built here rather than at any other place in the surrounding countryside, because at this place the hills on the horizon are sufficiently close to provide orientations to the midwinter and midsummer sunrises and sunsets even in poor visibility. Because of this, the Tump is not only a harvest hill - it is a solar observatory - just like Stonehenge.

Five thousand years ago, standing here on this mound, you would have seen the midsummer sun rise precisely over Cliffe Hill round barrow only three quarters of a mile away. At sunset you would have seen the sun god disappearing over the Blackcap barrows just three miles distant. At Alban Arthan, at midwinter, you would have seen the rebirth of the sun directly above the Beddingham Hill barrow, three and a half miles away, and its setting over Swanborough Hill barrow, two and a half miles away.

By positioning barrows and Tump in this way, the Druids or their forebears of old created here amongst the Sussex Downs, amongst the Slopes of the Galedin, a sun-clock of immense accuracy: a green clock-face of the Green King, as Rodney Castleden has called it.

By marking the Tump with a spiral path, its creators engraved in the very earth the symbol of the sun-god: for here, as at Glastonbury Tor where the spiral is of earth too, or as at Tintagel and New Grange where the spiral is carved in rock, we find the echo of the legend that the Sun-king, on his death, travels to a spiral castle. It is here, in this spiral castle, that the Sun-king, and all departed souls, gather before journeying through the Otherworld.

Not only was this solar observatory a sacred platform for offering up to the gods the first fruits of the harvest, it may well also have been a Hill of Excarnation - a sacred hill upon which those who had died were offered up to the Sky God. If this offering occurred on a physical level, then funeral pyres would have been built atop the mound, with the bodies being carried processionally around the spiral path in symbol of the journey of the soul in the Otherworld. This would explain why the mound was built just outside the boundaries of the town. But whether or not the bodies were actually carried to the top of the mound, it seems clear that such mounds act as subtle places of transfer between two worlds - this and the next.

I thought of the way in which visiting the Tump after hearing of Boris' death triggered this journey, and of how at Lucie's death I had felt drawn to the Tump again. At Sillustani, near Lake Titicaca in Peru, you can almost see the pale forms of departing souls gathering at the summit of a hill that looks exactly like Silbury, and which has a stone circle nearby. This mysterious mound is surrounded by water. And here too, as at Silbury, there would have been water.

At Silbury Hill the surrounding moat is 1100 feet long and fills with water regularly once each year. Michael Dames in his book *The Silbury Treasure*, suggests that this moat defines an image of the Great Mother, whose full womb is depicted by the hill itself. This image of the pregnant Harvest Mother was not static - but changed with sun and moon light. Dames tells us that if we go there at Lughnasadh we will see the moon rising over a nearby spring and striking its first light on the moat at exactly the place where you would expect a child's head to emerge:

> Then as the night goes on, this flicker of moonlight moves around the Mother, onto her knee, and crosses a narrow natural causeway of undisturbed chalk before filling up progressively a 'child' moat - a little disconnected piece of moat which is hugged tight against the belly mound of the hill itself; and the moon goes on through the night and eventually sets on the breast, so that the last moonlight you see is a flicker of white on the breast.

Here, as at Stonehenge and New Grange, we see the Ancients using the moving power of light in conjunction with the apparently static power of earthworks to create an effect worthy of the most sophisticated theatrical lighting engineers. Dames believes this effect of the moonlight was used deliberately to create a 'kinetic representation of the harvest birth.'

Flickering light and solid earth were united to demonstrate the paradox that in death there is life and in life death: that as the corn dies there is a new birth, new life. They are not separate realities, opposing states - they both exist within and because and as a part of each other. On such harvest hills and at the harvest time of our lives we celebrate the dying of the corn, the fulfilment of our lives, as we also celebrate the goddess's new birth, the baking of the first loaf, the beginning of a new cycle.

Down on the valley floor, the Brookland basin, as the sun was turning red in the darkening sky, I could see that the harvest had already begun. To watch this was strangely moving. But this sense of being moved changed to one of discomfort. A voice kept saying to me 'The harvest is not only for the land, it is for you and me - for all of us.' I closed my eyes and tried to determine where this sense of discomfort was coming from. I began to feel it as a call, a call that as I listened demanded that I allow myself to be dismembered - dismantled in some way. And as I allowed this demand to become more and more present within me, I felt more and more uncomfortable. In the end it felt as if my body and soul were being taken apart piece by piece.

And this was the call of the Harvest, this was the call of Lughnasadh. Here, at the age of forty, I should have been the happiest man in the world: our new baby had come to join us in the world, I had four of the loveliest children one could ever hope for: each one happy and loving and in good health. My second book was almost complete - two other books were about to be commissioned, I had my own office, offered by a friend and miraculously turning out to be right next to the Tump. And yet here, now, was nothing but dissolution and dismemberment. The accomplishments and achievements and joys of mid-life meant nothing to me any more. The seed which had for all this time provided me with such joy and pleasure as it sought release into this world was spent

- thoughts of making love and of sensual joy, or of making books and making friends no longer held any promise.

I lay back on the grass of the Tump, and finally surrendered to the threshing god. As I did this, in my inner vision there floated the images of all those I had hurt and loved, all those from whom I had taken and to whom I had given, all those I have known who have died and who will die, including myself and all my children, and all the children of the world.

And as this happened I could hear the moan of the combine harvesters working across the fields. It sounded as if they were all coming towards me, here on this hill, in the dying sunlight.

And then a voice whispered in my ear: 'When is it necessary to die?' and I found myself replying before I could even think clearly: 'When the flailing god comes unto me and says: "I shall tear you into a thousand pieces and scatter your body across the land".'

'Do you really want this to happen?' asked the soft voice beside me.

'No, of course not,' was my answer.

'Well, know this,' said the voice, which dropped in tone, 'that to stay his hand is to delay your death, but it is also to delay the time when your soul, like Isis, shall walk the earth gathering your body, piece by piece, until the moment when all the pieces shall be reunited and you shall become one again. And she, gazing into your being shall know that she has come to see herself at last, just as in gathering the shattered pieces of a mirror together, one comes at last to gaze upon one's own form.'

Hearing this, I let go. I allowed the combine harvesters to roll over me, the scythes to cut through me. Death was no longer a cloaked skeleton holding a scythe, but a happy farmer skimming his way through the wheat-sea. I could be happy too - I just had to let him do it. 'But they're mine!'

I shouted at him as his scythe bore down on me. 'They're my children, my books, my life!' But he just laughed at me, shouting back 'All you've ever wanted to do is make things: make love, make children, make books. Now you've made them and they're no longer yours!' And with that he cut a swathe through the wheat and as he did so, I was no longer sure whether the wheat was my body or my soul or the things I had made or none of these.

Then there was a lapse of time, a dreaming-space in which I lost myself and then found myself again. Then there was another voice, but this time it was the voice of Nuinn: 'Look over there - to the fields,' he said. And as I looked there was no longer a row of combine harvesters working its way across the landscape, but instead a group of peasants, gathered around a man - who was clearly their chief. With a sickle this man cut the first sheaf of corn, and held it high in the air, offering it to the god Lugh, before turning it three times around his head, chanting a blessing and an invocation for the protection of the tribe and its crops.

His chanting became a song and this song told of the beauty of the earth and the sky, the animals and the hills, the woods and the open sea. It asked that the land be held sacred and that the crops grow tall. It asked for the protection of the spirits and for the blessing of the goddess.

As I sat watching the setting sun, the scene faded and I was alone again. But I knew in my heart that I had heard one of the songs of our ancestors. And I knew too that this was also one of the songs of our children, being sung as our world enters its own time of harvest.

TORS

Earth to air, rock into sun
earthskin flowered in mauve and yellow
lionpeaks and lionwalks skirted in growth:
windsculpture above the downland, and the fringe
of low thick trees with the streams deep-threading.

Our headlands are always the crouching of beasts
guarding thick breasts of ebullient land:
fierce northern tigers, wildcats of wind
or stormy elephants that are many-legged,
watchful mild horses snuffing the gales,
rocky tops with the touches of creatures.

Earth into air, wind-lashed.

And the horses conceive of the wind
shaggy-haired pony foals are born.
Elephants stand in the tors,
wildcats cry in them.
The northern tiger and the lion lie
supine but watching........

They watch for the renewal of time
the coming of Arthur again, for strength
that breaks out of hiding and lashes
the skins of the ungodly: for the Great Light
that comes without lighting, that man has not made.

Rock seeks upward to the fire of sun
blown of the endless wind,
refreshed at the roots by water.
But the thunderbolt comes
that flashes from east even to west
that strikes where it will.
Indeed it has destroyed:
but where it has struck, there the Graal is made.

Nuinn

Appendix One

The Sacred Landscape of Sussex

Sussex is a dangerous place. It is the most goblin-haunted part of Britain: thirteen names in the county derive from pucca, which means goblin. Thanks to the Waste of Ondred, whose wolves, bears and brigands curbed northern missionary zeal, Sussex was the last part of Britain to become Christian: it was not until the late seventh century, 687CE, that the entire populace was converted. It is where the devil's wife is buried (at Devil's Dyke), where the last of the fairies to survive in Southern England live (at Harrow Hill, near Burpham), and where the dragons of Knucker Hole or St Leonard's Forest might eat you up, or where the giants of Firle, Caburn or Windover might challenge you to a stone hurling contest. And it is where the Sussex panther still roams – some say near Lewes at Kingston, others near Billingshurst. And it is where the ghostly sound of the bronze-age trumpet, the dord, can be heard near Battle.

Sussex is the second most wooded county in England (after Surrey) and has managed to preserve magnificent ancient woodland. It was home to Conan Doyle, Tennyson, HG Wells, Rudyard Kipling, Hilaire Belloc, Thomas Paine, Eric Gill, Burne-Jones, Elgar, John Evelyn, Richard Jefferies and Virginia Woolf. .

In the account that you have just read, I mention and visit only a small proportion of the many magical spots in this landscape. In the years that followed the publication of this book I discovered more places, and was told of more by participants in five workshops held in Lewes entitled 'The Sacred Landscape of Sussex'. As a consequence I have been able to expand the walk described in this book to include other sites:

At Eastbourne head for Holywell, the furthest point west along beach. Here, in the Italian Garden, you can watch the crowning of the May Queen and Morris dancers on May Day. Continue up to Beachy Head. Admire the view, and visit Whitbread Hollow, but ignore the ghost of a lady in grey and a monk in black, who are both said to beckon people over the cliff-edge.

Join the South Downs Way (see http://www.nationaltrails.gov.uk/southdownsframeset.htm) and follow it until you come to Avronelle, (Wilmington) and find barrows, the base of a windmill, the Long Man, a two thousand year old Yew Tree in the village church, and a good pub – The Giant's Rest. If you arrive at one of the eight festival times, you may find a group of Druids celebrating beside the Long Man or in The Giant's Rest (see www.bardicarts.com/anderidagorsedd/anderidahome.htm and www.giantsrest.free-online.co.uk).

Detour off the South Downs Way to the smallest church in an ancient grove at Lullington. Further on take tea in the strangely wistful Lullington Gardens which seems to exist in another dimension. Then cross Snake River (the Cuckmere) to walk up to the chalk horse at High & Over.

Then rejoin the South Downs Way at Alfriston. See its church built on a barrow. The churches in all these villages were also built on or by ancient mounds or barrows: Berwick, Up Marden, Falmer, Wilmington, Rottingdean, and St.John sub Castro in Lewes.

From Firle Beacon look down at, or visit Charleston (see www.charleston.org.uk) and across to Glynde, the Gill Giant and Mt Caburn. Pass tumuli and Red Lion pond and descend via Itford Hill to cross over the River Isis (Ouse).

Detour from the South Downs Way to visit Monk's House, Virginia Woolf's home.

Near Ditchling Beacon, in Stanmer Park, there used to be

a stone circle (most of the stones are now in 'Granny's Belt' an elongated copse in the park, which is private property). The circle was apparently destroyed in 1945 for farmland reclamation. At Buckland Bank between Stanmer Park and Lewes are the remains of a cursus in the landscape, near St.Mary's farm. Hollingbury Camp and Whitehawk Camp in the area are both worth visiting (stones from a circle at Whitehawk are now apparently lost under the racecourse stands, and standing stones once stood within the enclosure at Hollingbury, and probably where the Steine now is in Brighton, and at Bishopstone, in the Templar church at Shipley, and at Gold Stone in Hove Park).

On Ditchling Beacon wish or witch hounds are sometimes seen racing overhead here, chasing the souls of the 'damned', and the road between Ditchling and Westmeston, on Black Dog Hill, is haunted by a phantom headless black dog.

South of Hurstpierpoint you can see Wolstonbury Hill, and another Goddess in the landscape, like the fat-bellied woman of Lewes and the goddess at High and Over.

Perhaps it's the devil's wife? She is rarely mentioned as being in England, but at Devil's Dyke, just outside Brighton, the devil is said to have buried his wife in two mounds.

Continue along the South Downs Way, over the Adur and on to Chanctonbury Ring. Here you find a prehistoric fort and dykes, a destroyed burial mound and the site of a Roman temple. The devil appears if you run seven times backwards around the trees at midnight on Midsummer's Eve - he will then kindly offer you soup, milk or porridge. The trees are magically uncountable, like the Rollright stones, but if you guess the right number you'll raise the ghosts of Julius Caesar and his army. If you manage to avoid seeing Caesar or the devil, you might instead hear the hooves of invisible horses, and see the ghost of a bearded Druid searching for treasure.

Detour south to Cissbury Ring, which is a hill fort containing treasure guarded by two snakes or dragons. Antler picks were found in mine tunnels here dated to 3500 BCE. Fairies dance here at midnight on Midsummers Eve.

West of here are the mysterious Clapham Woods, and we are moving into dragon country now. South of the Way at Lyminster was the home of the Knucker dragon, and in the village church you can see the tomb of Jim Puttock, the local hero who killed the dragon. Very deep pools, known as 'Knucker holes' which may have had dragon inhabitants, were in Worthing, Shoreham and Lancing. Further north, at Dragon's Green just east of Billingshurst, was the home of Hilaire Belloc. And further north still we come to Rooster Pool in St.Leonard's Forest, home to another dragon, and home too, to mysterious caves.

The South Downs Way continues through forest now, passing north of the Trundle near Goodwood – a Neolithic causewayed camp and Iron Age hill fort. There buried treasure is guarded by a ghostly calf, which is sometimes heard bleating.

As the Way continues through Graffham Downs, Linchball Woods and Harting Woods, to the South is Kingley Vale – an area of majestic and mysterious ancient woodland containing a magnificent yew forest, and four round barrows, known as the devil's humps or kings' graves. Some say that viking chieftains are buried in these mounds, others that the devil could also be raised here by running round the barrows seven times. Others say the ghosts of warriors, or Druids, haunt the area.

Further west, at Felpham, on the coast south of Chichester, William Blake witnessed a fairy funeral, writing: "I was walking alone in my garden, there was great stillness among the branches and flowers and more common sweetness in the air; I heard a low and pleasant sound, and I knew not whence it came. At last I saw the broad leaf of a flower move, and underneath I saw a progression of creatures of the size and colour of green and grey grasshoppers, bearing a body laid out on a loose leaf, which they buried with songs, and then disappeared. It was a faery funeral."

If you continue along the South Downs Way you eventually come to Winchester, and can then follow the Clarendon Way to Salisbury, and then on to Stonehenge.

If you look at a map of Sussex you will see that I have described a selection of sites in just one part of the county – predominantly along the South Downs. There is still the rest of the county to explore: the Levels, the Weald, the coastline, and Sussex is just one of eighty-six counties in Britain. Each county, and each locality within each county, is rich in folklore, history and natural beauty.

APPENDIX TWO

RITES OF PASSAGE

In the story of the journey from Lewes to Wilmington and back, I include the text of a funeral service conducted in the Spring for Lucie Worthington.

For many of us, we are so overwhelmed by the death of someone close that we often allow the funeral service to be conducted by a priest whom often we have never met, and who has little or no knowledge of the person for whom they are conducting the service. Sometimes the result can be a service which is moving and profound, but more often than not the result seems inadequate and impersonal. In England, anyone can conduct a service at a crematorium, but there are constraints: only twenty minutes or so are allowed and everyone is seated in rows. Even so, within these limitations, there is time for us to express our sadness, wish the traveller on the Great Adventure well, and ask that they be blessed and guided on their journey.

Although the ceremony for Lucie was written specially for her, there are themes within it which are basic to a Druidic or spiritual understanding of the meaning of death. By taking these themes and weaving through them words appropriate to the life and circumstances of the person who has died, such a ceremony could be used for others. No special qualifications are needed to write or conduct such a ceremony - the important thing is that it is written and conducted from the heart by someone who knew the person.

The essential mystery of death is that it seems to be a separation - a parting - and yet we can never be parted from that which we truly love. But in an everyday sense it is of course a parting: of the soul from the body and of the loved one from our company, and this is why an alternative name for a 'funeral service' can be a 'parting ceremony'.

We wish those we love farewell in a Parting Ceremony - farewell in the sense that we wish that they might fare or journey well as they travel beyond the gateway to the Isles of the Blessed - or *Hy Breasil* as the Druids named these magical isles off the west coast of Britain.

In a Naming Ceremony, we greet a newly arrived soul who has travelled the other way: to earth. Here is the ceremony that Cairisthea and Will Worthington wrote and conducted one Spring morning on Iona, for our daughter Sophie when she was three months' old:

A Naming Ceremony

Stephanie and I, as parents, were asked to stand in the East. The dozen or so friends and relatives stood in a circle, and Sophie was carried by her godfather (if she had been a boy he might have been carried by his goddessmother). Sophie, in Nigel's arms, was outside the circle, in the West. Chris turned outwards to Nigel, saying:

"Who seeks entry into our world?"

Nigel replied: "One who has travelled the great wheel of death and rebirth many times and whose time has now come to return to the physical world."

Cairisthea spoke to Sophie, saying: "From the West out of the womb of the Great Mother we welcome you little one." As Nigel stepped through the Western gateway into the circle, Will spoke:

"We greet you and thank those who guide you for your safe return into this world. I give you the blessing of the Solar Father who seeded you; the blessing of the Great Mother who gave you form; and the blessing of Iona - that her strength and tranquillity might be always with you."

Cairisthea bathed Sophie's forehead in water drawn from the Well of Eternal Youth high up near the summit of Dun-I, saying: "I give you the name that will be with you throughout your journey." Will then said "There are others also who wish to welcome you." Slowly Sophie was carried clockwise around the circle by Nigel. Cairisthea held a small box open in her hands. Each member of the circle gave their greetings to Sophie, and placed in the box a token: a little gift - a stone or flower or poem. As Sophie reached us, we too greeted her and placed our gift, before she was carried from the East round the next half of the circle to the West again.

Then, from the West directly to the East, Nigel carried Sophie, flanked on either side by Cairisthea and Will. As Sophie was handed to us, Cairisthea said:

"We hand you, Sophie, into the safe-keeping of those who brought you to birth in the physical world: May the Great Ones guide and bless them."

This simple ceremony had the most extraordinary power. Just as Lucie was wished fare-well by walking from East to West in the ceremonial circle, so Sophie was greeted and wished well by carrying her in the reverse direction: from the West to the East. We come and go from the Isles of the Blessed in the West, and in our coming and going we celebrate our life to come and our life that has been. We ask for guidance and blessing whether our journey be in this world or the next.

Marriage

For some of us, our journey through life will include marriage - whether or not we choose to formalise our relationship legally or symbolically through a wedding or hand-fasting ceremony. Making use of material from earlier sources, including a Breton Druidic wedding, Cairisthea, together with Nicholas and Laura, wrote the following Druid Wedding ceremony which was celebrated for Jane and Michael with their friends and relatives and conducted by members of the Northern Grove of the Order of Bards Ovates & Druids in Lancashire:

A Wedding Ceremony

In this ceremony, the participants form both a circle and a horseshoe. At Jane and Michael's wedding, at a small stone circle, twelve participants formed an inner circle, standing by each of the twelve stones, with the rest of those present forming an outer horseshoe. In a different location, the reverse might apply, with a larger outer circle containing a smaller horseshoe-shaped group of participants.

Once both circle and horseshoe are formed, the Druid and Druidess, who will supervise the rite enter. The Circle is cast by the Druid and blessed and consecrated by the Druidess. They then say "Welcome!" and all reply "Welcome!"

The Gates are then opened by those at the Quarters:

Druid: Let the four directions be honoured that power and radiance might enter our circle for the good of all beings.

North: With the blessing of the great bear of the starry heavens and the deep and fruitful earth, we call upon the powers of the North.

South: With the blessing of the great stag in the heat of the chase and the inner fire of the sun, we call upon the powers of the South.

West: With the blessing of the salmon of wisdom who dwells within the sacred waters of the pool, we call upon the powers of the West.

East: With the blessing of the hawk of dawn soaring in the clear pure air, we call upon the powers of the East.

Druidess: May the harmony of our circle be complete.

Druid: We stand upon this Holy Earth and in the Face of Heaven to witness the Sacred Rite of Marriage between

Michael and Jane. Just as we come together as family and friends so we ask for the Greater Powers to be present here within our Circle. May this Sacred Union be filled with their Holy Presence.

Pause

By the power vested in me I invoke the God of Love whose name is Aengus mac Og to be present in this Sacred Place. In his name is Love declared.

Druidess: By the power vested in me I invoke the Goddess of the Bright Flame, whose name is Brigid to be present in the Sacred Place. In Her name is Peace declared.

Druid: In the name of the Ancestors whose Traditions we honour,

Druidess: In the name of those who gave us Life,

Both: May we all unite in Love.

Druidess: The joining together of Man and Woman in the Sacred Rite of Marriage brings together great forces from which may flow the seeds of future generations to be nurtured within the womb of Time. Within every Masculine nature lies the Feminine, within every Feminine nature lies the Masculine. The interplay of Masculine and Feminine forces when flowing freely in a union based upon true Love finds many expressions. This union is truly Holy.

Druid: Goddess to God,

Female Participant 1: God to Goddess,

Male Participant 1: Priestess to Priest,

Female Participant 2: Priest to Priestess,

Male Participant 2: Woman to Man,

Female Participant 3: Man to Woman,

Male Participant 3: Mother to Son,

Female Participant 4: Son to Mother,

Male Participant 4: Daughter to Father,

Female Participant 5: Father to Daughter,

Male Participant 5: Sister to Brother,

Druidess: Brother to Sister.
Druid: Who walks the Path of the Moon to stand before Heaven and declare her Sacred Vows?

Jane steps forward

Do you Jane come to this place of your own free will?
Jane: I do.
Druidess: Who walks the Path of the Sun to stand upon this Holy Earth and declare his Sacred Vows?

Michael steps forward

Do you Michael come to this place of your own free will?
Michael: I do.

Both walk the paths of the sun and moon
[clockwise and anti-clockwise]
around the circle, returning to the East.

Druid: Michael and Jane you have walked the Circles of the Sun and Moon, will you now walk together the Circle of Time, travelling through the Elements and the Seasons?
Jane & Michael: We will.

Walk hand in hand to South

South: Will your love survive the harsh fires of change?
Jane & Michael: It will.
South: Then accept the Blessing of the Element of Fire in this the place of Summer. May your home be filled with warmth.

Walk together to West

West: Will your love survive the ebb and flow of feeling?
Jane & Michael: It will.
West: Then accept the Blessing of the Element of Water in this the place of Autumn. May your life together be filled with love.

Walk together to North

North: Will your love survive the times of stillness and restriction?
Jane & Michael: It will.
North: Then accept the Blessing of the Element of Earth in this the place of Winter. May your union be strong and fruitful.

Walk together to East

East: Will your love survive the clear light of Day?
Jane & Michael: It will.
East: Then accept the Blessing of the Element of Air in this the Place of Spring. May your marriage be blessed by the Light of every new Dawn.
Druidess: All things in Nature are circular - night becomes day, day becomes night and night becomes day again. The moon waxes and wanes and waxes again. There is Spring, Summer, Autumn, Winter and then the Spring returns. These things are part of the Great Mysteries.
Michael and Jane, do you bring your symbols of these Great Mysteries of Life?
Jane & Michael: We do.
Druid: Then before all present repeat these words.
Jane *(facing Michael and handing him the ring)*: Accept in freedom this circle of gold as a token of my vows. With it I pledge my love, my strength and my friendship. I bring thee joy now and for ever. I vow upon this Holy Earth that through you I honour all men.
Michael *(facing Jane and handing her the ring)*: Accept in freedom this circle of gold as a token of my vows. With it I pledge my love, my strength and my friendship. I bring thee joy now and for ever. I vow in the face of Heaven that through you I honour all women.
Jane: In the name of Brighid I bring you the warmth of my heart *(Jane is handed a lighted taper by her mother or female participant)*.

Michael: In the name of Aengus mac Og I bring you the light of my love. *(Michael is handed a lighted taper by his father or male participant).*

They both light a single candle together. (This candle could be kept and relit at each anniversary)

All: May the warmth and the light of your union be blessed.
Druid: Do you swear upon the Sword of Justice to keep sacred your vows?
Jane & Michael: We swear.
Druidess: Then seal your promise with a kiss.
Druid: Beneficent Spirits and Souls of our Ancestors, accept the union of your children. Help them, guide them, protect and bless their home and the children born of their union. May their life together reflect the harmony of all life in its perfect union. May they work together in times of ease and times of hardship, knowing that they are truly blessed. From this time forth you walk together along Life's Path; may your way be Blessed.

Jane and Michael walk together sunwise around the circle to be greeted by each of the participants, then stand together west of centre.

Druid: It is the hour of recall. As the fire dies down let it be re-lit in your hearts. May your memories hold what the eye and ear have gained.
Druidess: We thank the Powers of Love and Peace for their presence within this Sacred Place.
Let us offer the words that unite all Druids:
Grant, O God/dess, thy Protection
And in protection, Strength
And in Strength, Understanding
And in Understanding, Knowledge
And in Knowledge, The Knowledge of Justice

And in the Knowledge of Justice, the Love of it
And in the Love of it, The Love of all Existences
And in the Love of all Existences, the Love of the God/ess and all Goodness.

Druid: Let the spirits of the Four Directions be thanked for their blessings.

East: In the name of the hawk of dawn and of the element air, we thank the powers of the East.

West: In the name of the salmon of wisdom and the element of water we thank the powers of the West.

South: In the name of the great stag and of the element of fire, we thank the powers of the South.

North: In the name of the great bear of the starry heavens and of the element of earth, we thank the powers of the North.

Druid: May the blessing of the Uncreated One, of The Created Word and of the Spirit that is the Inspirer be always with us.

Druidess: Let us now form the Three Circles of Existence. *(The married couple hold hands, forming the central circle. The participants in the outer circle and the horseshoe hold hands to form two further circles).*

All: We swear by peace and love to stand
Heart to heart and hand in hand
Mark O spirit and hear us now
Confirming this our Sacred Vow.

Druid: This Sacred Rite of Marriage ends in peace, as in peace it began. Let us withdraw, holding peace and love in our hearts until we meet again.

(The Druid unwinds the circle and exits sunwise. Michael and Jane follow. Then the rest of the inner circle. Then the outer circle walk across the centre in pairs and out through the western gate).

The Holy Grail

The marriage of two people symbolises the coming together of two apparently separate worlds, two apparently separate beings. It is highly appropriate that Lughnasadh, the time of harvest, should also be the time of marriage - for with marriage we allow our own individual lives to be harvested. We let go of our separateness and open to a new quality of life - one in which each partner is hopefully able to enjoy the fruits of each other and the relationship. One of the delights of marriage, and of love, is the discovery that our boundaries are fluid and changing - is this me? Is this you? Where do I end and you begin?

The greatest surprise in making the journey from the Tump to Wilmington and back, was that there too the boundaries between myself and the land, between past and present-day events, between inner and outer worlds, between the concrete and the imaginal, started to shift and change.

At the beginning of this book, I mentioned that the finding of the Holy Grail can be seen in terms of combining knowledge with inner experience. In making the journey, I discovered that one way to effect this combination is to physically walk the earth in such a way as to unite a knowledge of the land, its legends, its history, its geography, with an experience of it which is bodily and emotional, instinctual, imaginative and intuitive. The wonderful paradox is that by journeying in this way, in the country, in nature, we discover that NATURE ISN'T JUST OUT THERE!

"You only have to let the soft animal of your body
love what it loves.
Tell me about despair, yours, and I will tell you mine.
Meanwhile the world goes on....

Whoever you are, no matter how lonely,
the world offers itself to your imagination,
calls to you like the wild geese, harsh and exciting -
over and over announcing your place
in the family of things."

NOTES

The Druid Tradition

Druidry is not a complicated path. Appreciating it involves reorienting oneself so that one can approach the mysterious, the feminine, the Arts, both aesthetic and esoteric, in a way that allows us to let go of our assumptions and presumptions about life and instead carries us, as in a Druid ceremony, around the circle of our life towards the still point at the centre of which is both our True Self and the Divine Source.

from *Druid Mysteries – Ancient Wisdom for the 21st Century*

For introductory books on the Druid path, see *The Principles of Druidry* by Emma Restall Orr, Thorsons 1998, *Druids – A Beginner's Guide* by Caristhea Worthington, Hodder 1999, *A Guide to Druidry* by Philip Shallcrass, Piatkus 2000, and *Druid Mysteries – Ancient Wisdom for the 21st Century* by Philip Carr-Gomm, Rider 2002. Each book is short and easy to read, and includes practical exercises. Although they are introductory, they are written by people with years of experience in Druidry, and each one contributes something unique to an understanding of what Druidism is, and how it can be of value to you.

To learn more about Druidry, the internet is a powerful resource. Just type in 'Druidry' or 'Druid' into a search engine and a wealth of sites will be offered. As always with websites discrimination is needed - there are many wonderful sites, but also ones that may not be worth viewing. The Order of Bards Ovates & Druids' website at http://druidry.org has over a thousand pages of information that includes a library, a guided journey and meditation, sections on Druid camps, the Sacred Grove Planting Programme, the Campaign for Ecological Responsibility, training in Druidry, a bookshop, and comprehensive links to many other sites.

The Order of Bards Ovates & Druids runs an experience-based home-learning course. Each month teaching material is mailed to you, and you have the support of a mentor with whom you can write or email. In addition there are workshops, camps and celebrations in Britain and the USA and other parts of the world, and over ninety groves and seed-groups where you can meet and work with other members. The course is also available in various foreign language editions. Full details from: OBOD, PO Box 1333, Lewes, East Sussex, BN7 1DX. Tel/fax 44 – (0)1273 470888 Email office@druidry.org or see http://druidry.org (An audio version of this book may also available from OBOD).

To explore the work of Nuinn (Ross Nichols), a biography, photos, and selections of his paintings and poetry can be seen on http://druidry.org Also see:

The Book of Druidry by Ross Nichols, Thorsons 1990.

In The Grove of the Druids – the Druid Teachings of Ross Nichols by Philip Carr-Gomm, Watkins 2002.

To explore the ideas of sacred pilgrimage see www.gatekeeper.org.uk

For details of the open Druid festivals held eight times a year beside or near the Long Man see www.bardicarts.com/anderidagorsedd/anderidagorsedd.htm

Poems cited

'Wild Geese', published in *Dream Work* by Mary Oliver, copyright Mary Oliver 1986, appears with permission of the Atlantic Monthly Press.

'Shaman', published in *Transformation – The Poetry of*

Spiritual Consciousness edited by Jay Ramsay (Rivelin Grapheme Press 1988), appears with kind permission of Stephen Parr.

The poems of Nuinn are published in *Prophet, Priest & King - The Poetry of Philip Ross Nichols*, edited and introduced by Jay Ramsay (Oak Tree Press 2001). Available from OBOD.

Chapter Notes

Chapter Three

Hilaire Belloc, *The Old Road*, Constable & Co., 1911.

H.J.Massingham, *Through the Wilderness*, Cobden-Sanderson, 1935.

James Hillman and Michael Ventura, *We've Had a Hundred Years of Psychotherapy and the World's Getting Worse*, Harper SanFrancisco, 1992.

Chapter Four

René Guénon, *Le Roi du Monde*, Gallimard, 1958.

John Michell and Christine Rhone, *Twelve-Tribe Nations and the Science of Enchanting the Landscape,* Thames & Hudson, 1991.

Chapter Five

Rodney Castleden, *The Wilmington Giant*, Turnstone Press, 1983.

Chapter Six

Caitlin Matthews, *Mabon & The Mysteries of Britain*, Arkana, 1987.

Alfred Watkins, *The Old Straight Track*, Methuen, 1925.

Chapter Eight

Bryony and John Coles, *Sweet Track to Glastonbury: the*

Somerset Levels in Prehistory, London, 1986.
John Michell, *New Light on the Ancient Mystery of Glastonbury*, Gothic Image, 1990.
For an excellent survey of British prehistory, see James Dyer, *Ancient Britain,* Batsford, 1990.

Chapter Nine

I first heard the sound of bronze-age horns being played in New Grange during the first of a series of programmes on Early Scottish Music made for BBC Radio Scotland. The creator of this thirty-part series, John Purser, has also written a book *Scotland's Music* (Mainstream Publishing 1992) which includes illustrations of both these horns and the bronze rattles described.

The Barbican Museum by the castle in Lewes houses an excellent display of the finds from the Itford Hill farm site, including a chalk phallus (although not the one found during excavations under the main roundhouse's doorway) together with artists' impressions of the roundhouses. The illustration of the farm shown on the map accompanying this book shows artistic license: the main roundhouse depicted draws its inspiration from Durrington. A huge Celtic head recently found in a local garden rockery is also on display in the museum, together with a large model of a roundhouse and other interesting exhibits.

Chapter Ten

For an account of John Aubrey's connection with the English Druid Revival see Philip Carr-Gomm *Druid Mysteries – Ancient Wisdom for the 21st Century*, Rider 2002. For a study of Merlin's Prophecies see R.J.Stewart *The Prophetic Vision of Merlin*, Arkana 1986.

Chapter Eleven

The account of Eddius Stephanus, St.Wilfrid's chaplain,

is quoted in Rodney Castleden, *The Wilmington Giant,* Turnstone Press, 1983.

Chapter Twelve

Tom Graves, *Needles of Stone Revisited*, Gothic Image, 1986.
Marian Green, *A Harvest of Festivals*, Longman, 1980.

Chapter Thirteen

Robert Graves, *The White Goddess*, Faber & Faber, 1961.
Jean Huston, *The Search for the Beloved*, Crucible 1990.
Paul Kline, *Fact & Fantasy in Freudian Theory*, Methuen, 1972.
John Layard, *A Celtic Quest*, Spring Publications, 1975.
The Mabinogion, trans. J.Gantz, Penguin, 1976.
Michael Poynder, *Pi in the Sky*, Rider, 1992.
Claude Levi-Strauss, 'The Structural Study of Myth', in *Structural Anthropology,* Basic Books, 1958.

Chapter Fourteen

Francis Carr, *Who Wrote Don Quixote?* Xlibris, 2004.
Peter J.French, *John Dee - The World of an Elizabethan Magus*, Routledge & Kegan Paul, 1972.
N.T.Mirov and J.Hasbrouck, *The Story of Pines,* Indiana University Press, 1976.
To learn more about the Ogham tree alphabet see:
The Celtic Tree Oracle – a set of cards and a book which works with the sacred trees of the Celts and Druids. Liz & Colin Murray. Rider. 1989.
Celtic Wisdom Sticks – a bag of Ogham staves and a book which explains their oracular use. Caitlin Matthews, Connections 2001.

Chapter Fifteen

For details of the chalk horses and other figures to be found in Britain see Morris Marples, *White Horses and other Hill*

Figures, Alan Sutton Publishing 1981, and Paul Newman, *Lost Gods of Albion – the Chalk Hill-figures of Britain*, Sutton, 1999.

The John Matthews article can be found in *Psychology & The Spiritual Traditions* ed. R.J.Stewart, Element Books, 1990.

Results of research by The Dragon Project are given in Paul Devereux, *Places of Power – Measuring the Secret Energy of Sacred Sites*, Cassell, 1999.

Chapter Seventeen

Versions of the Mabinogion include the Lady Charlotte Guest translation published by Llanerch, 1989; the J.Gantz translation published by Penguin, 1976; and the Gwyn and Thomas Jones translation published by Dragon's Dream B.V., 1982.

For analysis of the tales' meaning see: Caitlin Matthews, *Mabon and the Mysteries of Britain*, Arkana, 1987 and *Arthur and the Sovereignty of Britain*, Arkana, 1989.

Chapter Eighteen

Brian Bates, *The Way of Wyrd*, Century, 1983.

Chapter Nineteen

For details of nineteenth and twentieth century authors' appreciation of nakedness, see Cec Cinder, *The Nudist Idea*, The Ultraviolet Press, Riverside, California, 1998.

For details of the connections between Naturism and Druidism see the section of this name at http://druidry.org

Margaret Gelling, *Signposts to the Past - Place-Names and the History of England*, Phillimore 1988.

John Bleach, A Romano-British (?) barrow cemetery and the origins of Lewes in *Sussex Archaeological Collections* 135 (1997), 131-42.

Richard Coates, *Some Place-Names of the Downland Fringe*, Younsmere Press 1990.

There are other less well supported theories as to the origin of the name Lewes. Perhaps, suggests Camden, it derives from the word *gluis* meaning bright or shining, or from *leaw* meaning an arm or hand. Lewis in Scotland is said to mean 'a hand in water' and Camden suggests that Lewes could have evolved from *Leaw-Ese* or *Lew-Ys* the Ese or Ys being the Isis, now the Ouse, towards which the town seems to reach like an arm or hand. Although no association is made in Place-name literature between Lewes and Lugh, it is interesting to note that the name of the Celtic god of Light, Lugh (and the related deity Lleu) is pronounced 'Loo' as in Lewes ('Loois') and that the Lewes Tump seems to have been a focus for the celebration of the old Celtic festival of Lughnasadh - Lugh's day. As guardian of the spear of Gorias, Lugh was also known as Lugh of the Long Arm, and it was he who was particularly associated with the first harvest as consort of the goddess of abundance. The first harvest was celebrated at the beginning of August on sacred mounds, such as the Tump, and if the town's name did not derive from Lugh, it is wonderfully fortuitous that his name can be heard echoing from Saxon times onward reminding us that this is indeed one of his sacred places - a place with a *hlaew*, a sacred mound that honours the Earth Mother and her consort Lugh of the Long Arm.

The quotation from T.Wright's *The History of Ludlow* 1841 mentions sacred mounds being frequently the scenes of popular ceremonies and meetings. Lewes' Lughnasadh connection was all but lost until Rodney Castleden's *The Wilmington Giant* appeared. But the town also has a connection with another of the Celtic quarter-day festivals, Samhain, between 31 October and 2 November, in the sense that in England in many ways this celebration now occurs on 5 November since it has become conflated with Guy

Fawkes' night. Lewes on 5 November becomes an almost pagan town - with thousands of visitors pouring into the narrow streets to watch torchlit processions, blazing tar barrels being thrown into the Ouse, and massive firework displays occurring simultaneously at four locations around the town.

Iolo Manuscripts - *A selection of Ancient Welsh Manuscripts*, published by the Welsh Manuscript Society, Llandovery MDCCCXLVIII. (see also *The Barddas* of Iolo Morganwg, with an introduction by John Matthews, Weiser Books, 2004).

Another reference to the Galedin is to be found in Iolo's collection of 'The Triads of Britain':

> There were three refuge-seeking tribes that came to the Isle of Britain; and they came under the peace and permission of the tribe of the Cambrians, without arms and without opposition. The first was the tribe of Caledonians in the north. The second was the Irish tribe, who dwell in the Highlands of Scotland. The third were the people of Galedin, who came in naked vessels to the Isle of Wight, when their country was drowned, and where they had land granted them by the tribe of the Cambrians.

(From *The Triads of Britain* compiled by Iolo Morganwg with an Introduction and Glossary by Malcolm Smith published by Wildwood House 1977.)

The translator of these triads from the Welsh in c. 1823, W.Probert, suggested that the Galedin came from Holland, although a later triad talks of the origin of certain other people being 'the border declivity of Galedin and Siluria'.

Chapter Twenty

Maire MacNeill, *The Festival of Lughnasa*, Oxford University Press, 1962.

For a more complete description of the Tump as a solar

observatory, together with diagrams, see Rodney Castleden *The Wilmington Giant*, Turnstone Press, 1983.

Michael Dames, *The Silbury Treasure*, Thames & Hudson, 1976.

See also his discussion with P.L.Travers in P.L.Travers, *What the Bee Knows - Reflections on Myth, Symbol and Story*, Aquarian 1989. The book opens with an old English adage: 'Ask the wild bee what the Druids knew.'

Revised Acknowledgements for the First Edition

This book is about a journey not only in space but also in time. As I walked the old trackways, I discovered that the actual events of the physical walk that I took became inextricably linked to the other events in my life during the nine months of writing and walking. 'Inner' and 'outer', 'real' and 'imaginary' experiences became in their turn woven into the historical, geographical and psychological research that was necessary as I undertook the journey.

I would like to thank everyone who helped or hindered the taking of this journey and the writing of this book. Those who hindered it are the closest to my heart and were really of the greatest help: my wife Stephanie, my niece Marianna and my children Matthew, Lawrence, Sophie and Charlotte. Every time I was dragged from my desk by bouncing children or domestic duties the book itself was creating the time to grow and mature in ways that were constantly surprising.

Special thanks are due to my son Matthew for suggesting that we carry bags of earth up to repair the damage to the Tump ourselves, and to Barbara Cole, who introduced me to Rodney Castleden's *The Wilmington Giant*, which has been such an inspiration for this book. I would also like to thank Nuinn, my old Druid mentor, for the inner guidance I received, and for his poems which I have used in the text;

Mary Oliver and Stephen Parr for allowing me to use their poems; my father for talking to me about his Don Quixote researches at precisely the right moment and for his term 'quintessentially Quixotic'; Dwina Murphy-Gibb for her insights as we talked about the Long Man and her wonderful support and encouragement in the difficult final stages of writing; the staff of the Sussex Archaeological Society's library; two friends whom I first met on the Tump: Andy Stirling who showed me the Iolo Manuscript and shared with me his ideas on Lewes and the surrounding area, and Jonathan Tait who introduced me to the work of Brian Bates; Cairisthea Worthington and Nicholas and Laura Spicer for allowing me to quote from ceremonies they have written; Will Worthington for his illustrations to the first edition; Stephanie Hirschmann for her research; Walter van Rijn who pointed out the sheep tracks and the leaping man of the chalk pit; Jackie Huxter who helped clarify for me the concept of Excarnation Hills; Phoebe and John Roper who kindly let me finish the book in their flat which faces the Tump; my psychotherapy clients who with such synchronicity have contributed images and ideas which have helped me to understand the journey of this book and the wider journey which we all take; Susan Henssler, Peter Hopkins, Harriet Green and Graeme Tallboys for their invaluable comments on reading the draft manuscript; Susan Mears who must be the most patient editor in the world; and all the friends and members of the Order of Bards Ovates and Druids whose conversations and letters have provided a constant stream of warmth and inspiration.

Acknowledgements for the Second Edition

I would like to thank two people for pursuing me: firstly the publisher Tom Clarke who with charm, persistence and humour persuaded me to add this title to his growing list of books that are written, not for the mass market, but for a serious and dedicated readership. Thoth Publications specialises in books written by British magicians, such as Dion Fortune, W.E.Butler, Gareth Knight, Melita Denning and Osborne Philips, Marian Green, John & Caitlin Matthews, and R.J.Stewart. I feel privileged to join their company.

My second pursuer was equally persistent: I rejected her advances as often as I rejected Tom's. A little after *The Druid Way* was first published, Caroline Dorling who ran a New Age centre in Lewes, contacted me and asked me to run a workshop on the sacred landscape of Sussex, based on this book. I declined her offer, feeling that as a Londoner only recently arrived in Lewes, I was unqualified. After several invitations over a year or so, I finally agreed, and we both found that there was such an interest in the subject that the workshop had to be held five times over. At each of these workshops I asked participants about their favourite places, and noted the stories they told about their experiences, and the history and folklore they had learned about the area. My thanks go to all those participants, since everything that I learned from them has helped to improve this book and deepen my appreciation of living in Sussex.

A number of people have told me that after reading this book they felt moved to take the same walk across the land. Their enthusiasm has been heartfelt, and I would like to thank in particular one of these people, who has become a friend and colleague: Damh Smith who helps to run the office of the Order of Bards Ovates & Druids, and who co-facilitates the Sussex Druid group, the Anderida Gorsedd, who organise open Druid festivals at the Long Man. My thanks also to the Avronelle Seed group of the Order whose member, Julie Couzens, showed me her evocative story about the Lady Avronelle and her husband Wildenhelm that I mention in Chapter Twelve. My deep appreciation also to Cairisthea Worthington for her contribution of the Foreword

Other titles form Thoth Publications

LIVING MAGICAL ARTS
By R.J. Stewart

Living Magical Arts is founded upon the author's practical experience of the Western Magical Traditions, and contains specific teachings from within a living and long established initiatory line of British, French, and Russian esoteric tradition.

Living Magical Arts offers a new and clear approach to the philosophy and practice of magic for the 21st century, stripping away the accumulated nonsense found in many repetitive publications, and re-stating the art for contemporary use. This book offers a coherent illustrated set of magical techniques for individual or group use, leading to profound changes of consciousness and subtle energy. Magical arts are revealed as an enduring system of insight into human and universal consciousness, combining a practical spiritual psychology (long predating materialist psychology) with an effective method of relating to the physical world. Many of the obscure aspects of magical work are clarified, with insights into themes such as the origins of magical arts, working with subtle forces, partaking of esoteric traditions, liberating sexual energies, magical effects upon the world of nature, and the future potential and development of creative magic.

ISBN 978-1-870450-61-4

PYTHONESS The Life & Work of Margaret Lumley Brown
By Gareth Knight

Margaret Lumley Brown was a leading member of Dion Fortune`s Society of the Inner Light, taking over many of Dion Fortune`s functions after the latter`s death in 1946. She raised the arts of seership to an entirely new level and has been hailed with some justification as the finest medium and psychic of the 20th century. Although she generally sought anonymity in her lifetime her work was the source of much of the inner teachings of the Society from 1946 to 1961 and provided much of the material for Gareth Knight`s The Secret Tradition in Arthurian Legend and A Practical Guide to Qabalistic Symbolism.

Gathered here is a four part record of the life and work of this remarkable woman. Part One presents the main biographical details largely as revealed by herself in an early work Both Sides of the Door an account of the frightening way in which her natural psychism developed as a consequence of experimenting with an ouija board in a haunted house. Part Two consists of articles written by her on such subjects as Dreams, Elementals, the Faery Kingdom, Healing and Atlantis, most of them commissioned for the legendary but short lived magazine New Dimensions. Part Three provides examples of her mediumship as Archpythoness of her occult fraternity with trance addresses on topics as diverse as Elemental Contacts, Angels and Archangels, Greek and Egyptian gods, and the Holy Grail. Part Four is devoted to the occult side of poetry, with some examples of her own work which was widely published in her day.

Gareth Knight was a colleague and friend of Margaret Lumley Brown in their days in the Society of the Inner Light together, to whom in later years she vouchsafed her literary remains, some esoteric memorabilia, and the privilege of being her literary executor.

ISBN 978-1-670450-75-1

PRINCIPLES OF HERMETIC PHILOSOPHY

By Dion Fortune & Gareth Knight

Principles of Hermetic Philosophy was the last known work written by Dion Fortune. It appeared in her Monthly letters to members and associates of the Society of the Inner Light between November 1942 and March 1944.

Her intention in this work is summed up in her own words: "The observations in these pages are an attempt to gather together the fragments of a forgotten wisdom and explain and expand them in the light of personal observation."

She was uniquely equipped to make highly significant personal observations in these matters as one of the leading practical occultists of her time. What is more, in these later works she feels less constrained by traditions of occult secrecy and takes an altogether more practical approach than in her earlier, well known textbooks.

Gareth Knight takes the opportunity to amplify her explanations and practical exercises with a series of full page illustrations, and provides a commentary on her work

ISBN 978-1-870450-34-8

* * * * *

THE STORY OF DION FORTUNE

As told to Charles Fielding and Carr Collins.

Dion Fortune and Aleister Crowley stand as the twentieth century's most influential leaders of the Western Esoteric Tradition. They were very different in their backgrounds, scholarship and style.

But, for many, Dion Fortune is the chosen exemplar of the Tradition - with no drugs, no homosexuality and no kinks. This book tells of her formative years and of her development.

At the end, she remains a complex and enigmatic figure, who can only be understood in the light of the system she evolved and worked to great effect.

There can be no definitive "Story of Dion Fortune". If incomplete, this retrospect provides an insight which provides understanding of her service to her times and ours, Readers may find themselves led into an experience of initiation as envisaged by this fearless and dedicated woman.

ISBN 978-1-870450-33-1

PRINCIPLES OF ESOTERIC HEALING

By Dion Fortune. Edited and arranged by Gareth Knight

One of the early ambitions of Dion Fortune along with her husband Dr Thomas Penry Evans was to found a clinic devoted to esoteric medicine, along the lines that she had fictionally described in her series of short stories The Secrets of Dr. Taverner. The original Dr. Taverner was her first occult teacher Dr. Theodore Moriarty, about whom she later wrote: "if there had been no Dr. Taverner there would have been no Dion Fortune!"

Shortly after their marriage in 1927 she and Dr. Evans began to receive a series of inner communications from a contact whom they referred to as the Master of Medicine. Owing to the pressure of all their other work in founding an occult school the clinic never came to fruition as first intended, but a mass of material was gathered in the course of their little publicised healing work, which combined esoteric knowledge and practice with professional medical expertise.

Most of this material has since been recovered from scattered files and reveals a fascinating approach to esoteric healing, taking into account the whole human being. Health problems are examined in terms of their physical, etheric, astral, mental or spiritual origination, along with principles of esoteric diagnosis based upon the structure of the Qabalistic Tree of Life. The function and malfunction of the psychic centres are described along with principles for their treatment by conventional or alternative therapeutic methods, with particular attention paid to the aura and the etheric double. Apart from its application to the healing arts much of the material is of wider interest for it demonstrates techniques for general development of the psychic and intuitive faculties apart from their more specialised use in assisting diagnosis.

ISBN 978-1-870450-85-0

PRACTICAL OCCULTISM

By Dion Fortune supplemented by Gareth Knight

This book contains the complete text of Dion Fortune's *Practical Occultism in Daily Life* which she wrote to explain, simply and practically, enough of the occult doctrines and methods to enable any reasonably intelligent and well balanced person to make practical use of them in the circumstances of daily life. She gives sound advice on remembering past incarnations, working out karma, divination, the use and abuse of mind power and much more.

Gareth Knight has delved into the Dion Fortune archive to provide additional material not available before outside Dion Fortune's immediate circle. It includes instruction on astral magic, the discipline of the mysteries, inner plane communicators, black magic and mental trespassing, nature contracts and elemental shrines.

In addition, Dion Fortune's review of *The Literature of Illuminism* describes the books she found most useful in her own quest, ranging from books for beginners to those on initiation, Qabalah, occult fiction, the old gods of England, Atlantis, witchcraft and yoga. In conclusion there is an interpretation by Dion Fortune's close friend Netta Fornario of *The Immortal Hour*, that haunting work of faery magic by Fiona Macleod, first performed at Glastonbury.

ISBN 978-1-870450-47-8

THE FOOL'S COAT
By Vi Marriott

The story of Father Bérenger Saunière, the poor parish priest of Rennes-le-Château, a remote village in Southern France, who at the turn of the 19th century spent mysterious millions on creating a fantastic estate and lavishly entertaining the rich and famous, is now as well known as "Cinderella" or "Eastenders". He would never divulge where the money came from, and popular belief is that in 1891 he discovered a priceless treasure; yet Saunière died penniless, and his legacy is a secret that has continued to puzzle and intrigue succeeding generations.

Since *The Holy Blood and the Holy Grail* hit literary headlines in the nineteen eighties, hundreds of solutions have been suggested. Did he find documents that proved Jesus married Mary Magdalene? Was he a member of The Priory of Sion, a sinister secret society that knew the Da Vinci Code? Did he own the equivalent of Harry Potter's Philosopher's Stone?

A literary mosaic of history, mystery, gossip and myth, THE FOOL'S COAT investigates Father Saunière's extraordinary life against the background of his times, and suggests that the simplest solution of his rise from penury to riches is probably the correct one.

Vi Marriott is a theatre administrator, writer and researcher. Her play Ten Days A-Maze, based on Count Jan Pococki's Tales of the Saragossa Manuscript, had seasons in London and Edinburgh; and she contributes regularly to three "house" magazines concerned with the mystery of Rennes-le-Château and other esoteric matters.

ISBN 978-1-870450-99-7

THE GRAIL SEEKER'S COMPANION
By John Matthews & Marian Green

There have been many books about the Grail, written from many differing standpoints. Some have been practical, some purely historical, others literary, but this is the first Grail book which sets out to help the esoterically inclined seeker through the maze of symbolism, character and myth which surrounds the central point of the Grail.

In today's frantic world when many people have their material needs met some still seek spiritual fulfilment. They are drawn to explore the old philosophies and traditions, particularly that of our Western Celtic Heritage. It is here they encounter the quest for the Holy Grail, that mysterious object which will bring hope and healing to all. Some have come to recognise that they dwell in a spiritual wasteland and now search that symbol of the Grail which may be the only remedy. Here is the guide book for the modern seeker, explaining the history and pointing clearly towards the Aquarian Grail of the future. John Matthews and Marian Green have each been involved in the study of the mysteries of Britain and the Grail myth for over thirty-five years.

In *The Grail Seeker's Companion* they have provided a guidebook not just to places, but to people, stories and theories surrounding the Grail. A reference book of Grail-ology, including history, ritual, meditation, advice and instruction. In short, everything you are likely to need before you set out on the most important adventure of your life.

"This is the only book that points the way to the Holy Grail in the 21st century." *Quest*

ISBN 978-1-870450-49-2

THE DRUIDIC ORDER OF THE PENDRAGON
By Colin Robertson

The Druidic Order of the Pendragon reveals the rituals and secrets of a Druid order active in Derbyshire from the mid-nineteenth century until the 1940s. The author was sworn to secrecy during his lifetime but wrote down all his knowledge of the Order's ceremonials and symbolism for posthumous publication. He describes much that, but for his diligence, would be lost to a modern readership. There are surprisingly few parallels to other Druidical, magical or pagan groups. The initiation rituals are not for the faint-hearted and, to initiates, eggs will never seem the same again.

The Druidic Order of the Pendragon is a delightful insight into an all-but lost world of powerful self development. At a time when paganism is increasingly diluted by teen witches, this is a reminder that ritual magic can be an effective tool for personal change.

ISBN 978-1-870450-55-3